General Directory of Newry, Armagh, etc.,
for 1820

THE GENERAL DIRECTORY OF

NEWRY, ARMAGH,

AND THE TOWNS OF

Dungannon,	Banbridge,
Portadown,	Warrenpoint,
Tandragee,	Rosstrevor,
Lurgan,	Kilkeel,
Waringstown,	Rathfriland, &c.

FOR 1820;

CONTAINING

AN ALPHABETICAL LIST OF THE MERCHANTS,
MANUFACTURERS, AND INHABITANTS IN GENERAL;

AND

HISTORICAL ACCOUNTS

OF

THE RESPECTIVE TOWNS.

ALSO,

A LIST OF ENGLISH AND IRISH BANKERS.

BY THOMAS BRADSHAW.

 BooksUlster

First printed by Alexander Wilkinson, the *Telegraph-Office*, Newry, 1819. This new edition published by Books Ulster, 2017.

www.booksulster.com
www.libraryireland.com

ISBN   978-1-910375-64-8

Typographical arrangement © Books Ulster

The cover illustration is from an engraving of Narrow-water Castle, County Down, by William Henry Bartlett. Taken from *The Scenery and Antiquities of Ireland*, 1840.

Advertisement.

Having now completed a Second Part of my *General Directory for the North of Ireland*, I submit it to the Public, with a hope that my exertions will meet their approbation.—The Third Part shall appear early in the ensuing spring.

To my numerous Subscribers, and particulary to those who have favoured me with various historical accounts of the different towns and villages, I beg to return my most grateful thanks.

As I propose taking a Directory triennially, I look forward with confidence to that support which I have experienced from the commencement of my work.

THOMAS BRADSHAW.

Newry, December, 1819.

Contents.

DIRECTORY

OF

THE TOWN OF NEWRY,

AND THE

TOWNS ADJOINING,

FOR 1820.

Historical Account of the Town of Newry.

Newry is situated in latitude 54° 10′ north, and longitude 6° 16′ west. It stands on a small river, called the Newry Water, which has its source in Drumlough, near the town of Rathfriland, in the barony of Upper Iveagh. This river meets the tide at Newry, and forms the boundary between the counties of Down and Armagh.

Newry is 50 miles distant from Dublin, 30 from Belfast, and 14½ from Armagh. Formerly the principal part of the town stood immediately along the side of a steep hill, which stretches nearly north and south; but since its commerce became more considerable, in consequence of the improvements made in its navigation, the streets have extended in the direction of the river and canal. Since the river and tide have been confined by embankments, many good houses have been built on ground formerly flooded by the tide.

Charles Havern, a man of one hundred and eleven years of age, remembered when the Low Ground was altogether a marsh; and afterwards when there were two bleach-greens where the coffee-room now stands.

So late as the year 1700, Mill-street contained only six or seven slated houses. Market-street had a few of the same description; but the rest were merely thatched cabins. At this time the town was surrounded by woods. A large piece of timber was placed over the ford of Sugar-island, for the accommodation of foot passengers, by a person named Murphy. In consequence of this, the stone bridge afterwards built over the river, at this place, bore the name of *Mudda-Murphy-bridge,* or the bridge of Murphy's stick. It is a good bridge of five arches. Formerly there were ten arches; but five of them being of no use for venting the water, it was thought unnecessary to retain them.

The road through the town northwards formerly lay through Ballybot, Mill-street, Market-street and High-street, and united with the Banbridge road at Stream street. But latterly the line of road, has been much improved by a new cut, in the direction of the river, along the level between the turnpike and the Low Ground. The line to Rathfriland has also been improved by a cut more northward, which meets the Banbridge road at the end of the town. The old line runs through High-street, Church-street, and Pound-street.

Above the town, the former Dublin road was very steep and difficult for horses drawing, loaded cars and carriages. A considerable time ago, the line was much improved by a cut more west-ward, which has made the ascent more gradual and easy. The Dublin bridge, by which this road unites with the body of the town, was lately rebuilt, and rendered much handsomer than the old one.

A little below this bridge, there are some remains of a ford observable, by which there had formerly been a passage over the river, at low water.

The most considerable ancient establishment at Newry was the monastery, which deserves to be particularly mentioned on account of the subsequent appropriation of its privileges and possessions.

In the year 1157, an abbey of Cistercian monks, dedicated to St. Mary and St. Patrick, was founded at Newry, by Maurice Mac Loughlin, king of Ireland. But it is recorded, that in 1162, the abbey and a library connected with it, were consumed by fire—The endowments were confirmed by Hugh de Lacy, earl of Ulster, in 1237.

This abbey flourished until the reign of Henry VIII. who

changed its constitution into that of a collegiate church for secular priests, in the year 1543, at the suit of Sir Arthur Magenis, who was at the time knighted, and received £50 of the king's bounty. The college consisted of a warden and vicars choral. Henry granted to them a confirmation of all their possessions, in his thirtieth year, reserving to the crown a yearly rent of four marks.

The Latin name of the abbey was *Nevoracense Monasterium.* In the foundation charter, it is called *Ibar Cyn tracta,* that is, the flourishing head of a yew tree. The reason why it obtained this designation appears from an old tradition, that two large yew trees grew within the precincts of the abbey. From this circumstance, it was called, in the barbarous Latin of the age, *Monasterium de viridi ligno,* and in Irish, *Na Jur,* or the yew trees. This gave occasion to the plural appellation, by which it was afterwards most commonly known, *the Newries.* The authors of the old county Down survey, who wrote about the year 1740, state, that it "was still fresh in the memories of some ancient inhabitants of the town, that in the year 1688, certain English soldiers, in burying their dead, discovered, in the south-east quarter of the abbey, the stumps of some trees of fine wood; and without regard to the place, rooted up and converted them to several domestic utensils, the wood being red and bearing a fine polish."

This abbey was situated in Castle-street, at the head of the street which is opposite to the new church. Part of the building still remains, and is at present occupied as two dwelling-houses. The walls are extremely thick and strong; and the alterations in the building which have been made in modern times, were attended with unusual difficulty and labour. Within the last sixty years, there was a very massive stone stair-case outside the building. It was no easy task to take this down, owing to the extreme hardness and solidity of the work. It is said that the men employed found it necessary to blow it up with gunpowder.

Large quantities of human bones, some of them of very uncommon size, have been dug up at different times, both in front and rear of this edifice, a circumstance which proves that the ground contiguous to the abbey had been appropriated to the burying of the dead. About eighty or ninety years ago, a merchant of the town, on digging foundations within the precincts of the ancient abbey, found a human skeleton, seven feet in length.—Some remains of shoes, which bore the impression of buckles, and some remnants, probably of the shroud, were discovered.* Several fragments of stones, with heads and other figures rudely sculptured upon them, are to be seen in some of the adjacent buildings. These formerly belonged to the buildings of the abbey.

After Henry VIII. had disclaimed subjection to the papal see, the college was dissolved; and in the succeeding reign of Edward VI. the lordship was granted to Marshal Bagnal, who made the abbey his place of residence.

A mitred abbot formerly possessed the lordships of Newry and Mourne, in which he exercised episcopal jurisdiction. On the dissolution of the abbey, the powers and privileges enjoyed by the lord abbot devolved on the temporal proprietor, Sir Nicholas Bagnal, to whom a patent was granted by Edward VI. on account of his excellent services, as marshal of Ireland. He rebuilt the town, and strengthened it with castles and other defences. He also built the church, the steeple of which bears the Bagnal arms, cut in stone, dated 1578. Within its walls his remains were afterwards interred.

The patent granted to Sir Nicholas Bagnal expresses the nature and extent of the grant briefly, and principally in general terms. But the letters patent granted by James I. anno 1613, to Arthur

---

* It is said that formerly abbots and bishops were buried in their shoes.

Bagnal, Esq. are full and explicit, and recite particularly the townlands included in the grant, the privileges to be enjoyed, and the jurisdiction to be exercised within the manors. The proprietor being entitled to the several immunities and privileges enjoyed under the former ecclesiastical establishment, is permitted to use in his court the seal of the ancient charter, on which is represented a mitred abbot in his albe, sitting in his chair, supported by two yew trees, with this inscription— *Sigillum exemptæ jurisdictionis de viridi ligno, alias, Newry et Mourne.*

The patent grants to Arthur Bagnal, Esq. his heirs and assigns, the town of Newry, with all the demesne lands of the dissolved monastery—the manor, lordship and castle of Greencastle—the lordship, country or territory of Mourne, with two islands in the main sea—the manor of Carlingford, with the monastery and its appurtenances, and the lands of Cooley—the ferry between Carlingford and Killowen—the customs of anchorage, and certain customs of goods and merchandize imported into or exported from Carlingford—the territory of Omeath, and all wrecks of sea, happening upon these properties.

It grants a market at Newry, to be held every Thursday, with tolls, customs and commodities: also a custom or toll of six gallons from every butt of wine called sack, and three and a half gallons from every hogshead of wine sold in Newry; three gallons from every barrel of ale, and 4d. out of every barrel of salt—and the assize of bread and wine in the town of Newry.

It grants to the patentee, to hold, by his seneschal, a court at Newry, to determine causes of debt, trespass, &c. when the sum shall not exceed £66 13s. 4d. and also all the profits and fines appertaining to the said court.—It grants all fines and amercements which shall be imposed, assessed, adjudged and decreed at any assizes or sessions to be held in the county, upon any of the inhabitants of the manor.

It permits a court to be held at Greencastle, to hold pleas of actions, not exceeding forty pounds sterling; and a court at Carlingford for actions not exceeding £10.

It grants also a court baron to be held from three weeks to three weeks, to hold pleas of debt, tresspass, &c. not exceeding £40. Likewise a court-leet twice a year, in Newry and Mourne—together with all the profits, fines, &c, arising out of the same.

The patent further grants two fairs to be held at Newry yearly, each for three days; and at Greencastle a weekly market on Friday, and one fair in the year, with courts of pipowder—together with all the tolls and customs belonging to the same; requiring from the patentee 6s. 8d. yearly for the privilege of holding these markets and fairs, and of appointing the clerks of the markets.

The lord of the manors, it is said, can command the sheriff not to carry his rod of office through his domains even before the judges. He has power to discharge, by his receipt, all recognisances forfeited within his jurisdiction, if the offenders shall have resided therein six weeks prior to the forfeiture: and the sum forfeited he can order to be paid into his own treasury in lieu of the king's exchequer.

He appoints bailiffs, who serve writs, &c. so that no bailiff, sheriff, or minister of the crown shall enter on the manors, to execute and serve writs, &c. which ought to be executed or served therein, except for the default of those bailiffs.

By virtue of his patent, the proprietor is entitled to the tithes of the lordship of Newry, and has the right of presentation to the rectory of Mourne. He is *ex officio* rector of Newry; and, by his vicar general and surrogate, grants probates of wills, letters of administration, letters of tutelage, and marriage licenses, and transacts the usual business of an ecclesiastical court, with as plenary and indisputable powers as any other ecclesiastical court in Ireland. He appoints a vicar to discharge the ministerial duties, to whom he pays a salary. And as by virtue of his patent, he enjoys all episcopal powers, which can possibly vest in a layman, the vicar is responsible for his conduct to him alone, and is not subject to the jurisdiction either of bishop or primate.

After reciting the several particulars of the grant, the patent states, "And we do give, grant, bargain and confirm unto the said Arthur Bagnal, his heirs and assigns, all and singular and so many and the like court leets, frank pledge, law days, rights, jurisdictions, liberties, privileges, &c. in as large, ample, and beneficial a manner as any abbot, prior, or convent, or other chief head or governor of the late dissolved monastery heretofore seized, held or enjoyed," &c. So that all the privileges and immunities, of whatsoever kind, that formerly were enjoyed by the abbots of Newry, were transferred to the patentee, his heirs and assigns.

In King James's patent, there is an exception made of certain lands and tenements which had been granted by Sir Nicholas and Sir Henry Bagnal, (reserving, however, the tithes and royalties,) to Patrick Creely, of Newry, in fee farm, by indenture of feoffment, dated the 20th of June, 1588, and two water mills in the town of Newry, with the water-courses, &c. and also two wears in the river Clanrye, near the town, in which salmon and eels had been commonly taken. It appears that this Creely, in the reign of Queen Elizabeth, built the castle, afterwards called Lord Hillsborough's castle. He was bound to pay to Bagnal, his heirs and assigns, a chiefrie of £3 6s. 8d. per annum. This property, included in the townland of Cornehaugh, was purchased from the heirs of Creely by Mr. Hill, the ancestor of the present Marquis of Downshire.

The manors of Newry, Mourne and Carlingford, having been enjoyed by the Bagnal family, for upwards of a century, were latterly shared by two proprietors, Robert Nedham and Edward Bayly, in whom they vested by the will of their father-in-law, Nicholas Bagnal. In 1715, they were divided. The Down and

Armagh estates fell to Nedham, and the Louth to Bayly. Edward Bayly was greatgrandfather to the present proprietor, the Earl of Uxbridge. The next, Robert Nedham, on his decease, left two sons. George, the elder, sold part of the estate to enable him to discharge certain debts with which it was encumbered; having, for this purpose, procured an act of Parliament. William not having married, nor having any near male relations, left the estate by will to the predecessor of the present proprietor, Francis Needham, Viscount Kilmorey. His lordship's income, arising from the Newry and Mourne estates, amounts at present to about £15,000.

The town of Newry was reduced to a very ruinous condition in the rebellion of 1641. It was surprised by Sir Con Magenis, at the breaking out of the rebellion, and continued in his possession ten weeks, after which it was retaken by Lord Conway. At this time, the inhabitants suffered many grievous hardships.

After the restoration, the town was rebuilt, and improved considerably; till in 1689, it was burned by the Duke of Berwick, the better to enable him to secure his retreat before the English forces under the command of the Duke of Schomberg. The castle and five or six houses only escaped the conflagration.

The church was demolished in 1641; the walls and steeple, however, were suffered to remain. It continued in this ruinous state till after the restoration, when one half of the church, together with the vestry was covered. About the year 1720, the other half of it was repaired; and in 1729, the roof was taken off, and the walls raised six feet higher, to make room for a gallery. Around the church is the ground in which the Protestants of the town and its vicinity bury their dead.

It appears from King James's patent, that besides the church in the town there were two chapels connected with it, belonging to the parish, one called Templegiveron, and the other Castlelenegan.

The old church not being conveniently situated nor sufficiently large enough, a new one has lately been erected in a more convenient situation, and on a larger plan. The first stone of this church, which is named *St. Mary's,* was laid by the Rev. Charles Campbell, vicar of Newry, on the 17th of October, 1810. It was opened for Divine service on the 21st of November, 1819.

The church is built in the Gothic style, of excellent hammered granite, procured in the neighbourhood of the town. The size of the building within is 75 feet by 51, exclusive of the chancel. The height of the steeple and spire is about 190 feet.

The ancient Presbyterian meeting-house was situated at a place still called Meeting-house Rocks, near the turnpike, on the Belfast road, about three quarters of a mile from town. It was built probably about the year 1650.

The present commodious structure in High-street, was erected in the year 1722; excepting the south aisle, which was added about forty years afterwards. In the meeting-house yard, there is an excellent dial, made by Adams, of London, and presented to the congregation by Mr. Robert Wallace, of Croban, in the year 1757.—It appears, that, for a considerable time prior to the revolution, and after it, the congregation had for minister, the Rev. George Lang, of Carnmeen. The next minister was the Rev. Robert Rainey, who continued in the charge till 1739. The Rev. James Moody, who had been previously minister of Maherally, succeeded, and died in 1772, having been minister forty years. The Rev. Boyle Moody, his son, having succeeded to the charge, died in February, 1799. His successor, the Rev. John Thom, who had been invited from Scotland, became minister in 1800, and died in July, 1808. The Rev. A. G. Malcom, D. D. great grandson of the Rev. George Lang, and also kinsman of the Messrs. Moody, was installed in March, 1809. He had previously been minister of the congregation of Dunmurry.

The number of families belonging to the Presbyterian congregation, amount to nearly 400.

The present Catholic chapel is situated at that extremity of Boat-street, which is now denominated Chapel-street, on a rising ground, at the bottom of which the former chapel had stood. It was built in 1789, and the inhabitants of Newry, of all religious denominations, contributed very liberally to it. It is a large, well-built house, with three galleries, and has a spacious burying ground connected with it, part of which was given by the late Lord Kilmorey. The former cemetery, and the most ancient Catholic chapel of the town were situated in Boat-street, at the place now occupied as a potato-market. This chapel was that which appertained to the monastery; and some remains of it were standing about eighty years ago. On opening the street and levelling the ground at this place (a thing which occasioned murmuring) great heaps of human remains were displaced, of which large quantities were carried away and deposited in the present Catholic burying ground. Much of the earth raised on this occasion was taken to fill up a large hollow between Boat-street and the Dublin bridge.

The ground for the new chapel was given by Mr. Nedham; and the present Lord Kilmorey presented the parish with a handsome organ, which is now used by them in public worship.

Doctor Lennan left £30 a year to a clergyman to perform divine service in the chapel of Newry every day, for ever. Mr. Fitzsimons, of Newry, also bequeathed an equal sum for the same purpose; so that every day there are two services in the chapel, and on Sundays and holidays three.

Opposite to the chapel is a Catholic school-house, built about fourteen years ago. Dr. Lennan had left £600 in the 5 per cents, to endow the school, with permission to his executors to subtract £100 from it toward building a school-house. The executors, however, not wishing to break the original sum, succeeded in building a good school-house by other means.

There is a meeting-house of Seceders of the associate synod, situated off Church-street, with a burying ground adjoining. Mr. Nedham gave the ground for 6*d.* a year rent. The first congregation of Seceders was formed hereabout the year 1750.

In William-street there is a Methodist chapel, which has lately been made a very comfortable place of worship. The present preachers are, the Rev. George Stephenson and the Rev. Edward Cobain.

The old custom-house, a very good building, is situated on the river, opposite to what was formerly the lowest lock of the canal. It has latterly been occupied as a fever hospital. The present custom-house stands on the Merchants'-quay, and is a plain building. Lately, extensive and well-built stores have been erected in the adjoining yard.

The court-house is situated in Hill-street, and was formerly a market-house, built by private subscription. But no lease having been procured, it became the property of the Downshire family. It was altered into a sessions-house about the year 1805. Though in a central situation, it is, at present, rather injurious to the appearance of the street in which it stands, being an awkward old building. If it were removed, and bridges erected over the river and the canal, opposite Margaret-street, a considerable improvement would be thus effected in that part of the town.

The sessions-house in Ballybot has a good gaol connected with it. The only place of confinement in the County Down side, consists of two small cells under the Boat-street market-house.

The house containing the news-room and ball-room was built by some gentlemen of the town and neighbourhood, in 1794. A variety of newspapers and other publications are read at the news-room. The room is furnished with an excellent Atlas and barometer, a gazeteer, army and navy lists, &c. &c. Exchange is held in it every Thursday. It is open for all strangers. The rent and other charges are defrayed by the annual contributions of the subscribers.

The theatre was built by Mr. Betterton, about the year 1783, by subscription. Tickets of admission were granted to the subscribers, according to the sums subscribed. But an ejectment for non-payment of rent having issued, the property of the subscribers was lost.

The present barrack was built by a company of gentlemen, originally for a white linen-hall. The design not having succeeded, the concern was sold to government for about one-third of what it had cost, which was about £14,000. The buildings are remarkably well adapted to the uses to which they are at present applied. It is thought, that they could not have been better planned, even if they had at first been designed for a military purpose. Their proximity to the canal is a great advantage. They are equal to the accommodation of 1144 men. There is, however, a separate barrack for the officers in the street called Corry-place.

The old butter-crane was situated in Boat street. The place being too far distant from the canal, and otherwise incommodious, the late Lord Kilmorey erected a new one on the canal, at Ballybot bridge, which is large and convenient, and well adapted to the trade. A commodious corn market-house has also been erected in Ballybot.

On the 16th of August, 1813, a Lancasterian school was established in Newry, under the patronage of a number of ladies. On an average, 140 children give regular attendance. They are charged one penny a week for their tuition. The school is at present held in the room above the meal market-house; but the inhabitants of Newry look forward to a much more perfect establishment for the education of the poor.

A work school for the benefit of female children has also been established by the ladies of Newry. A room was taken in Hide-street, and a mistress engaged, who attends three hours daily, to instruct the children in the several kinds of needle work.

About twenty girls, who attend the Lancasterian school in the morning, are taught in this place.

In the year 1809, a Reading Society was formed in Newry. Each member, besides the sum required on admission, pays one guinea per annum. This money is applied to paying a librarian and purchasing books.

In 1812, a Bible Society was established, forming a branch of the Hibernian Bible Society. Lord Kilmorey is president. The repository is at Surgeon Miller's, in Market-street.

In 1814, a Humane Society, for the recovery of persons apparently dead, was established. This was imperiously called for by the many afflicting instances of death occasioned by drowning, which had of late years occurred in Newry.—The society have purchased an excellent resuscitative apparatus, and have appointed a number of receiving houses in convenient situations. They have also published cards of instruction for restoring suspended animation.

A company, named "The Newry Amicable Annuity Company," was established in 1770. Its object is to provide an annuity for the widows of the members. At present the capital is upwards of £25,000; the number of members one hundred, and the number of annuities twenty-eight. The company pay, from year to year, whatever sum the interest of the capital, appears to authorize. At present the widows receive £56. The admission money and subscriptions go to the augmentation of the stock. The monies of the company are lent on private security; maiden mortages of lands only being accepted.

There are two classical schools at present in Newry, which are very well attended.

A public bakery has for some years been carried on in Newry, which has been of considerable utility in regulating the assize of bread.

There are at present two large distilleries in Newry. The old one, though not working at present, is one of the most complete concerns of the kind in Ireland. The distillery in Monaghan-street, is as perfect as possible, and produces excellent whiskey. In Ballybot, there are two extensive breweries, both of which are working at present.

Near Violet-hill there is an establishment for the manufacture of spades, shovels, and rod and hoop iron; and in Newry there is a foundry for casting brass and iron.

The consequence of the town of Newry, is best ascertained by its commerce. This is very considerable; and is partly to be attributed to the excellence of the navigation, and partly to the geographical situation of that town, which is naturally con-nected with several flourishing counties, particularly Armagh, Down, Monaghan, Louth, Cavan, Fermanagh and Tyrone.

The total tonnage invoiced yearly at the port of Newry, amounts to 40,000 tons.

The revenue of the port and district of Newry, yearly, in cus-toms, excise and stamps, amounts to 270,000*l.* the customs being taken at 123,000*l.* the excise at 125,000*l.* and the stamps at 22,000*l.*

The quantity of flaxseed imported, when the trade is open, is very considerable. On an average, it may be taken at 9,000 hogsheads, yearly.

Newry has a very considerable export of butter, provisions, and linen cloth. The export of the former, may annually be rated at 80,000 casks, averaging 3*l.* 10*s.* per cask. Besides this, there are from 1000 to 1200 crocks sold at the crane, for home consumption, averaging 1*l.* 5*s.* per crock.

From the first of October, 1813, till the first of July, 1814, there were exported from Newry, 1285 tierces of beef, 1960 barrels of pork, and 600 bales of bacon.

In 1814, there were exported 23,350 barrels of oats of 14 stone—4546 barrels of wheat of 20 stone—2760 packs and boxes of linen—2600 bales of flax, average weight, 4 cwt. 2 qrs.—3942 pigs, and 698 cows, besides sheep and horses, large quantities of feathers, bran, tanners' waste, horns, &c.—The entire export may be valued at one million annually.

It appears from the patent, that in the reign of James I. the town of Newry contained about 300 edifices. At present, the number may be stated to be about 2500, and the number of inhabitants 13,000.

The town has a very considerable market for linens, butter, flax, oats, pigs, potatoes, &c. The linen market at present averages about £5,000.

Newry has two fairs, and Ballybot, also called Southwark, may hold four in the year. The latter were obtained many years ago, at the instance of two considerable merchants named O Hear, but are not now held.

❧

Arrival and Departure of the different Mail and Stage Coaches.

The Belfast and Dublin Royal Day Mail starts from the office, No. 10, Castle-street, Belfast, every morning at 5 o'clock; breakfasts at Newry, and arrives at the Waterford Hotel, Sackville-street, at 7 o'clock in the evening; from whence it starts for Belfast, at 7 every morning, dines at Newry, and arrives in Belfast at half past 9 in the evening.

The Belfast and Dublin Royal Night Mail starts from the above office in Belfast, every day, at 4 in the afternoon; arrives in Newry at half past 9, and in Dublin, at the same office as the above coach, at 7 o'clock next morning; from whence it starts for Belfast at 8 o'clock in the evening, breakfasts next morning in Newry, and arrives in Belfast at 11.

The Lark Day Coach starts from Williams's Hotel, Newry, precisely at 7 o'clock every morning, breakfasts at Dundalk, and arrives in Dublin at 5 in the evening, at No. 6, Bolton-street; starts every morning at 7 o'clock for Newry.

The Armagh Coach starts from Mrs. Hillan's Hotel, Water-street, Newry, every evening, and leaves M'Kean's inn, Armagh, for Newry, at 6 o'clock in the morning.

The Downpatrick Coach starts from Mrs. Hillan's on the mornings of Mondays, Wednesdays, and Fridays; returns every Tuesday, Thursday, and Sunday, from Mr. Ward's, Downpatrick.

⌘

Conveyances by Water.

Three packets, *The St. Patrick,* Captain Whyley, *The Marquis,* Captain Hall, and *The Mary,* Captain Gooden, sail with passengers, &c. from Warrenpoint to Liverpool, and return alternately.

A few years ago, a passage boat was built by several gentlemen, to ply between Newry and Knock-bridge, on the Newry canal. It leaves Newry every Tuesday, Thursday, and Saturday, and returns every Monday, Wednesday, and Friday.

Directory of Newry, for 1819.

A

Abernathy, Henry, ladies' shoemaker, Canal street.

Adams, William, baker, North street.

Aiken, Andrew, merchant, Turner hill.

Aiken, Messrs. John, Son and Co. merchants, Merchants' quay.

Aickin, Graves, clock and watchmaker, Water st.

Alcorn, Jane, seminary for young ladies, Kildare st.

Alexander, Samuel, turner, Church street.

Allen, William, warehouseman, Drumalane.

Anderson, Rev. James, Needham place.

Anderson, Samuel, sawyer, Needham place.

Anderson, Samuel, jun, sawyer, Catherine lane.

Anderson, John, clothes-dealer, North street.

Anderson, Samuel, boot and shoemaker, North st.

Anthony, John, wheelwright, Pound street.

Atkins, Mrs. Elizabeth, Canal street.

Atkinson, Mrs. Arrabella, Boat street.

B

Baird, Hans, painter, glazier, oil and colour merchant, Hill street.

Baird, William, stonecutter, Courtney hill.

Ballard, William, coppersmith, North street.

Ballard, Mary, lodging-house, North street.

Ballentine, Hugh, nailor, High street.

Barr, John, cabinet-maker, Church street.

Barret, Hugh, saddler whip, and harness-maker, Sugar island.

Barret, T. R. constable, North street.

Baxter, Robert, tinman, Needham place.

Beath, William, Esq Boat street.

Bell, Samuel, gentleman, Hill street.

Bell, Edward, haberdasher, Hill street.

Bell, Mrs. Catherine, Needham place.

Bell, George Washington, surgeon and chymist, drug, spice, oil and colour warehouse, Hill st.

Benn, Robert, coachmaker, Hill street.

Benn, John, coachmaker, Basin.

Benn, Thomas, hat manufacturer, North street.

Bennett, Patrick, shoemaker, Canal street.

Bennett, Bernard, ditto, High street.

Bergan, Michael, engineer, Hill street.

Best, E. and J. grocers, Sugar island.

Best, William, dealer, Monaghan street.

Black, William, M. D. Church street.

Black, Thomas, apothecary, North street.

Black, Samuel, M. D. Marcus square.

Black, Adam, Shakespeare Tavern, Hill street.

Black, Archibald, slater, Hyde market.

Blacker, William, leather-seller, Courtney hill.

Blacker, Robert, clothes-dealer, North street.

Blackham, George, jeweller and silver-smith, watch and clock maker, Hill street.

Blackham, William, bookbinder and stationer, Hill street.

Blackham, James, saddler, Market street.

Blackham, Richard, bookbinder, Boat street.

Blackham, William, publican, Boat street.

Blaney, Mary, haberdasher, North street.

Bloxham, Richard, constable, North street.

Boland, Benjamin, coach-painter, Hill street.
Books, Patrick, salemaster, Hill street,
Boyd & Ker, merchants, Monaghan street.
Boyd, Samuel, merchant, Queen street.
Boyd, John & Hugh, merchants, Basin.
Boyd, Hugh, gent. Hill street.
Boyd, James, painter and glazier, North street.
Boyd, James, shoemaker, High street.
Boyd, John, shoemaker, High street.
Boyd, John, cardmaker, Pound street.
Bowes, James, carpenter, Boat street.
Boyle, Charles, nailer, King street.
Boyle, Michael, brass-founder, Basin.
Boyle, Patrick, butcher, Castle street.
Boyle, Matthew, teacher, Castle street.
Boyle, Henry, farmer, Pound street.
Boyle, Armor, salt-refiner and merchant, Old quay.
Brady, Thomas, grocer and spirit-dealer, Castle st.
Brady, Daniel, grocer and spirit-dealer, Castle st.
Brady, Andrew, thread manufacturer, High street.
Brady, C. and A. dressmakers, Canal street.
Branagan, Michael, baker, High street.
Brighton, Roger, huxter, Canal street.
Browne, Rev. Thomas, William street.
Brown, Surgeon, Staff, Canal street.
Brown, William, wine merchant, High street.
Brown, Robert, sen. cooper, Edward street.
Brown, Robert, jun. cooper, Edward street.
Brown, Thomas, tidewaiter, King street.
Brown, William, shoemaker, Stream street.
Brown, Jane, clothes-dealer, High street.
Brown, Samuel, slater, Boat street.
Brown, William, slater, Boat street.

Bryden, William, merchant, Canal quay.

Bryden, James, cabinet-maker, King street.

Burgess, James, excise officer, Catherine street, Canal street.

Burke, Edward, feather merchant, Boat street.

Burns, Peter, publican, Boat-street.

Burns, Thomas, hemp dresser, Church street.

Burns, James, flaxdresser, Boat street.

Burns, Patrick, cooper, Nicholson's row.

Butler, Sylvester, corkcutter, Lower Water st.

Byrne, Catherine, woollen-draper and leather merchant, Castle street.

Byrne, William, publican *Led Rion,* North-street

C

CADLEY, Thomas, leather-cutter, Mill street.

Cairns, Thomas, gardner, Drumalane.

Calaghan, James, hairdresser, Boat street.

Campbell, Rev. Charles, Boat street.

Campbell, Felix, publican, Boat street.

Campbell, Alexander, tax collector, Sugar island.

Campbell, E. & M linen drapers, North street.

Campbell, Eliza, schoolmistress, High street.

Campbell, Archibald, principal of the English and mercantile academy, High street.

Campbell, Hugh, shoemaker, Stream street.

Campbell, Thomas, pawnbroker, Castle street.

Campbell, Michael, publican, Canal street.

Campbell, Thomas, Hill street.

Campbell, James, shoemaker, Canal street.

Caragher, John, merchant, Merchants' quay.

Cargey, James, book-keeper, Kiln street.

Carlile; Hugh, merchant, Merchants' quay; house, Canal-street.

Carlile, Walter, shoemaker, High street.
Carr, William, shoemaker, Stream street.
Carr, Thomas, dealer in meal and flour, High st.
Carter, William, merchant, Canal street.
Casey, Hugh, brickmaker, Market street.
Cassidy, Terence, shoemaker, Hill-street.
Cassidy, Catherine, huxter, Hill street.
Caulfield, Dennis, distiller, Merchants' quay.
Caulfield, Dennis & Co. distillers, Monaghan street.
Caulfield, Edward, wholesale grocer and spirit merchant,
    Hill street.
Caulfield, Maria, haberdasher, Hill street.
Clark, James K. Lieutenant Royal Artillery, Sugar island.
Clark, James, warehouseman, Canal street.
Clark, Patrick, cooper, Boat street.
Clark, Arthur, auctioneer, High-street.
Clark, Edward, merchant, High street.
Clark, William, huxter, Courtney hill.
Clark, William, gardner, Boat street.
Cliveland, Elinor, seminary for young ladies, Hill street.
Cochran, Mrs. W. Monaghan street.
Coffay, John, huxter, Castle street.
Coleman, Bernard, tallow chandler, Boat street.
Collins, Catherine, grocer, Water street.
Collins, William, Water street.
Collins, Arthur, bluedier, North street.
Colligan, Edward, blacksmith, Hill street.
Conlin, Hugh, tanner, Lower Water street.
Conlin, Thomas, baker, Boat street.
Colvin, George, cooper, Canal street.
Conna, James, broguemaker, High street.
Connelly, Margaret, huxter, Castle street.
Connelly, Patrick, paver, Boat street.

Cooke, George, permit-officer, Canal street.

Cooke, George, jun. grocer and spirit-dealer, Canal street.

Cooke, Richard, merchant, Merchant's quay.

Copeland, William, publican, North street.

Copeland, Hamilton, salt-boiler, Market street.

Copes, Mary, publican, *Elephant,* Water street.

Corbett, John, public notary, Hill street.

Corbett, John, billiard-rooms, Hill street.

Corry & Little, merchants, Merchant's quay.

Corry, Mrs. Isaac, Courtney hill.

Corry, William Isaac, Esq. Boat street.

Corry, Trevor, Esq. Boat street.

Corry, William, miller, Marcus square.

Corry, Mary, milliner, Boat street.

Corry, Samuel, bookbinder and umbrella-maker, Market street.

Corry, Joseph, Boat street.

Corry, E. S. Boat street.

Cosgrove, Francis, dier, Mill street.

Cosgrove, Edward, farrier, William street.

Cosgrove, Richard, seaman, William street.

Cotter, Johnson, nailer, William street.

Courtney & Boyd, brewers and malsters, Queen street, Ballybot.

Courtney, Mrs. Mary, Queen street.

Courtney, Mrs. Ann, Basin.

Courtney, Mrs. E. William street.

Courtney, Sarah, huxter, North street.

Courtney, Miss Sarah, Courtney hill.

Cowan, James, architect and measurer, Mill street.

Cowan, William, grocer and flour-dealer, Market street.

Cowan, Joseph, farmer, Pound street.

Cowan, George, hat manufacturer, North street.

Cowden, James, cooper, Canal street.

Craig, Moses, cooper, King street.

Craig, Elizabeth, huxter, King street.

Crawford, Samuel, publican and cooper, Castle st.

Crawford, Hugh, publican, Boat street.

Crawford, Andrew, soap boiler and tallow chandler, North street.

Creevy, William, seedsman, Hill street.

Creek, William and James, hardware merchants, North street.

Crozier, Margaret, haberdasher, North street.

Cullen, Thomas, dealer, New street.

Cumings, John, custom-house officer, King street.

Cumings, Patrick, tidewaiter, Boat street.

Cunningham, Felix, jauntingcar-keeper, Courtney hill

Cunningham, Michael, currier and tanner, Hide market.

Cunningham, Eliza, hat manufacturer, North st.

Cunningham, Mary, huxter, Castle street.

Cunningham, Michael, hat manufacturer, Market street.

Cunningham, Elizabeth, publican and agent for the Liverpool packets.

Curran, Mary, midwife, Needham place.

D

DALY, Francis, publican, North street.

Davis, Archibald, Boat street.

Davis, Robert, ropemaker, Stream street.

Davidson, John, merchant, High street.

Davidson, John, cooper, High street.

Davidson, Isaac, grocer, Water street.

Davidson, Arthur, chandler and grocer, Water st.

Dempsey, James, huxter, Mill street.

Dempsey, John, publican, Castle street.
Derry, Right Rev. Dr. Edmund, Boat street.
Devlin, Mark, grocer and baker, Castle street.
Devlin, Bernard, reedmaker, Castle street.
Dogherty, Daniel, huxter, Boat street.
Dogherty, John, shoemaker, Church street.
Donnell, James, leather-cutter, North street.
Donnelly, John, cooper, Canal street.
Donnelly, James, gardner, Boat street.
Donnelly, Arthur, shoemaker, Boat street.
Doran, Edward, steward of Fever Hospital, Old quay.
Doran, Edward, nailer, Castle street.
Douglass, Wm. letter-press printer, Sugar island.
Douglass, Jane, straw hat manufacturer, Sugar island.
Downey, Hugh, butcher, Castle street.
Downey, Ann, baker, Castle street.
Downey, Michael, butcher, Castle street.
Downey, Francis, shoemaker, Catherine lane.
Downs, John, shoemaker, High street.
Doyle, Peter, cartmaker, Hide market.
Doyle, Patrick, cooper, Ballybot.
Duffy, Terence, coal merchant, New street.
Duffy, Laurence, cap & harness-maker, Queen st.
Duncan, Robert, weaver, Stream street.
Dunn, Michael, cattle and feather-dealer, Hill st.
Dunsheath, James, combmaker, High street.
Dunsheath, Mary, staymaker, High street.
Duplex, Henry, dealer, Boat street.

E

EDGAR, Joseph, ropemaker, High street.
Elliott, William, shoemaker, High street.
Eves, John, High street.

F

FARRELL, David, blacksmith, North street.

Fegan, Terence, grocer and wool merchant, High street.

Fegan, Margaret, butcher, Castle street.

Fegan, James, cardmaker, Market street.

Fegan, Maria, huxter, Mill street.

Fegan, Hugh, currier and tanner, Mill street.

Fegan, Edward, lighterman, Boat street.

Ferguson, George, engineer, Monaghan street.

Feran & Coleman, grocers, Water street.

Feran, Edward, innkeeper, *White Cross,* Water st.

Feran, Patrick, dealer, Mill street.

Feran, Felix, cow-keeper, High street.

Ferrigan, James, provision dealer, Mill street.

Ferrigan, James, butcher, Mill street.

Finnigan, Bryan, stone mason, William street.

Flanagan, William, tailor, High street.

Flanagan, John, cabinet-maker, Church street.

Flanagan, Catherine, dressmaker, William street.

Flanagan, James, nailer, Stream street.

Flavel, John, Mill street.

Fletcher, William, cabinet-maker and upholsterer, Kildare street.

Fletcher, Michael, gent. Canal street.

Fletcher, Isaac, cabinet-maker, King street.

Fitzpatrick, William, mason, Church street.

Fitzpatrick, Patrick, tobacconist, Church street.

Fitzsimmons, Frances, dressmaker, Basin.

Foster, John, shoemaker and clothes-dealer, North street.

Fox, Peter, eating-house, Canal street.

Fox, John, collar and harness-maker, Lower Water street.

Foxall, Mrs. Sarah, Boat street.

Frazer, George, deputy barrackmaster, Barrack.

Frazer, John, letter press printer, Barrack street.

Frazer, George, jun. pawnbroker, Canal street.

Fullerton, Thomas, reedmaker, High street.

G

GALAGHER, James, clothes-dealer, North street.

Gant, Samuel, shoemaker, Stream street.

Gibson, John, constable, Boat street.

Gillespie, William, currier, Boat street.

Giliespie, Hugh, currier, Boat street.

Gillespie, Townley, straw bonnet warehouse, Sugar island.

Gillespie, Andrew, mason, High street.

Glenn, Samuel, wheelwright, Boat street.

Glenny & Melling, merchants, Merchants' quay.

Glenny, Mrs. W. Hill street.

Glenny, Mary, clothes-dealer, North street.

Glenny, Isaac G. merchant, Castle street.

Glenny, William, merchant, Castle street.

Glenny, Joseph, solicitor, Courtney hill.

Godfrey, Camac, merchant, Merchants' quay.

Godfrey, George, ship-broker, New street, Canal quay.

Godfrey, Mrs. Elizabeth, North street.

Gordon & Parsons, flour merchants, *Temple Gowran*; stores, Trevor hill.

Gordon, William, brazier, &c. North street.

Gordon, Miss Hannah, Boat street.

Gossan, John, baker and spirit-dealer, Market st.

Gough, Patrick, huxter, Canal street.

Gourley, Samuel, reedmaker and clothes dealer, North street.

Graham, William, carpenter, High street.

Graham, Andrew, woollen-draper, Market street.

Graham, John, flaxdresser, Boat street.

Grandy, Henry, tailor, North street.

Grandy, Joseph, tailor, High street.

Grant, John, skinner, Hill street.

Grant, Laurence, farmer, Pound street.

Grant, Nicholas, grocer and spirit-dealer, Castle street.

Grant, Thomas, publican and butter-merchant, Merchants' quay.

Gray, Sarah, publican, *Coach and Horses,* Margaret street.

Grayson, John, cooper, Queen street.

Greer, Robert, solicitor, Hill street.

Greer, Willam,[*sic*] coach proprietor, Hill street.

Greer, Thomas, coach proprietor, Marcus square.

Greer, James, Hill street.

Griffin, John, mason, Kiln yard.

Griffin, Thomas, carpenter, Mill street,

Griffin, George, seaman, Canal street.

Griffin, Matthew, mason, Queen street.

Griffin, Philip, publican, Water street.

Guy, George, merchant, Merchants' quay.

Guy, George, Needham place.

Guy, John, boot and shoemaker, Needham place.

Guy, Mrs. Mary, William street.

Guy, John, shoe-maker, Mill street.

Guy, George, hosier, North street.

Guy, Robert, Boat street.

H

HAGAN, Matthew, wool-dealer, High street.

Haley, Francis, pipemaker, Market square.

Hall, Robert, distiller, Monaghan street.

Halyday, Arbuckle, Hill street.

Halyday, J. T. woollen and carpet warehouse, Hill street.

Halyday, James, Hill street.

Halyday, William, whitesmith, Canal street.

Hamil, William, paymaster's clerk, Barrack.

Hamilton, Major, staff officer, Corry square.

Hamilton, John, hairdresser, Hill street.

Hamilton, James, publican, Mill street.

Hamilton, Robert, tidewaiter, Dromalane.

Hamilton, William, shoemaker, High street.

Hammerton, Robert, permit officer, Barrack street.

Hancock, William, grocer, Sugar island.

Hancock, Robert, saddler and harness-maker, Margaret street.

Hanna, George, merchant, Canal street.

Hanna, John, carrier, Pound street.

Harbinson, Matthew, painter and glazier, High st.

Harcourt, Richard, grocer, High street.

Harcourt, James, farmer, High street.

Harris, James, whitesmith, Castle lane.

Harvey, Thomas, merchant, Trevor hill.

Harvey, Mrs. Mary, Hide street.

Harvey, Thomas, merchant, Merchants' quay.

Harvey, Thomas, Mill street.

Haughton, Alexander, shoemaker, Church street.

Haughey, John, architect, Hill street.

Haughey, Maurice, glass, china and earthen warehouse, Margaret street.

Hawkins, Charles, officer of customs, Needham st.

Heaney, Michael, chandler, High street.

Henderson, David, classical & mathematical school, Hill street.

Henderson, Andrew, hosier, High street.

Hennesy, John, chairmaker, Church street.

Henning, Joseph, tailor and habit-maker, Canal street.

Henning, Martha, straw hat manufacturer, Hill st.

Henning, Robert, lime-burner, Boat street.

Henry & Reid, merchants, Sugar-house quay.

Henry, Thomas, farmer, High street.

Henry, James, wheelwright, Boat street.

Heron, M. & C. haberdashers, North street.

Hill, James, merchant, Trevor hill.

Hill, Moses, carpenter, North street.

Hill, Joseph, wheelwright, Sandy street.

Hill, William, shoemaker, High street.

Hill, John, cooper, Church street.

Hill, James, coppersmith, Monaghan street.

Hillam, Harold, Boat street.

Hillan, Mary, hotel and tavern, Water street.

Hillan, Edward, mason, Boat street.

Hinchy, Patrick, coachmaker, Mill street.

Hind, David, blacksmith, Water street.

Hogg, William James, gent. Canal street.

Holmes, James, gent. Stream street.

Holmes, James, roper, High street.

Hopper, Thomas, shoemaker, Canal street.

Horton, Moses, publican, High street.

Hughes, Philip, merchant, High street.

Hughes, Mrs. Mary, Basin.

Humphreys, William, builder and carpenter, Boat street.

Hurst, Rev. John, Boat street.

Hutchinson, Andrew, shoemaker, New street.

I

Ingram, Joseph, carpenter, Boat street.

Ingram, John, carpenter, Boat street.

Irwin, James, officer of customs, Barrack street.
Irwin, William, gunsmith, Boat street.

J

JACKSON, Edward, plasterer, Boat street.
Jackson, William, accountant, Barrack street.
Jefferson & Godfrey, merchants and ship brokers, Merchants' quay.
Jefferson, Thomas, ship-broker, Barrack street.
Jefferson, Misses D. and M. A. Canal street.
Jennings, Charles, merchant, Merchants' quay.
Jennings, Daniel, spirit-dealer, Mill street.
Jennings, Peter, ironmonger, North street.
Jennings, Andrew, merchant, Merchants' quay.
Jennett, James, cardmaker, Catherine street.
Johnson, William G. merchant, William street.
Johnson, William, M. D. Turner hill.
Johnson, John, Courtney hill.
Johnson, Thomas, flaxdresser, High street.
Johnson, George, flaxdresser, High street.
Jordon, Thomas, carpenter, Church street.
Jordon, Samuel, carpenter, Church street.

K

KEAN, Edward, commissioner, Monaghan street.
Kean, William, rope-maker, Chequer hill.
Kean, Thomas, mason, Boat street.
Kearney, Patrick, Water street.
Kearney, John, huxter. Water street.
Kearney, Francis, farmer, Boat street.
Kearney, Peter, weaver, Kiln yard.
Kearney, Patrick, farmer, Boat street.

Kearney. Michael, flax-dresser, Boat street.

Keegan, Andrew, turner, Pound street.

Keenan, John, clothes-broker, North street.

Keenan, Bernard, blue-dier, North street.

Keenan, Patrick, tobacco-spinner, Church street.

Kelly, George, tailor and clothes-dealer, North st.

Kelly, Bernard, schoolmaster, High street.

Kelly, Patrick, dealer, Boat street.

Kenna, Thomas, shoemaker, Boat street.

Kennedy, Sarah, huxster, Mill street.

Kerr, Rev. John, Seceding minister, High street.

Kerr, Joseph, tobacco-spinner, Church street.

Kerr, James, shoemaker, Church street.

Kernaghan, Adam, butcher, High street.

Kernaghan, James, butcher, High street.

Killin, Thomas, publican, Mill street.

King, Thomas, grocer, North street.

Kindellan, Thomas, cooper, King street.

L

Lamb, James, comb-maker, Hide street.

Lang, William, ship-broker, Boat street.

Latty, William R. piano forte maker, tuner and repairer, North street.

Lawless, Henry, baker, Canal street.

Lawson, Francis, ship-broker, Boat street.

Leathem, Thomas, officer of excise, Ballybot.

Ledlie, Edward, soap-boiler and chandler, Canal st.

Lee, Isaac, schoolmaster, Mill street.

Lee, James, shoemaker, Mill street.

Lee, Susanna, upholsterer, North street.

Lemon, Alexander, boot and shoemaker, North st.

Lenaghan, William, gent. Bridge street.
Lennon, James, huxter, Mill street.
Leonard, Thomas, carpenter, Boat street.
Lester, James, soap-boiler and chandler, King st.
Lester, John, book agent, Boat street.
Liddy, Richard, hardwareman, North street.
Liggett, Hugh, nailer, Canal street.
Little, Archibald, merchant, Downshire road.
Linden, William, baker, Castle street.
Lock, John, shoemaker, Boat street.
Lockhart, James, carpenter, North street.
Lockhart, James, shoemaker, North street.
Logan, William, tailor, Bridge street.
Longford, John, livery servant, Boat street.
Lowry, Thomas, huxter, Merchants' quay.
Lowry, James, huxter, William street.
Luddon, John, tailor, Water street.
Lutton, Thomas, weaver, Church street.
Lutton, John, shoemaker, Castle street.
Lyle, Joseph, merchant, Merchants' quay.
Lyle, James, pawn-broker, High street.
Lynes, Patrick, huxter, High street.
Lynes, Patrick, huxter, Canal street.

M

MACKAY, John, salt-maker, Canal street.
Madden, Hugh, weaver, church street.
Madill, Robert, whitesmith and ironmonger, Canal street.
Magee, John, tailor, Ellis's entry, Lower Water st.
Magee, John, carpenter, Hill street.
Magennis, Felix, linen-draper, Mill street.
Magennis, Thomas, ship bread baker, Market st.
Magennis, Thomas, baker, North street.

Magennis, Mary, Bridge street.

Magennis, Roger, slater, King street.

Magennis, Hugh, card-maker, Water street.

Magill, Edward, coachman, Lower Water street.

Magill, Henry, huxster, High street.

Magaffin, James, surgeon and apothecary, North st.

Maguire & M'Parlan, merchants, Merchants' quay.

Maguire, Hugh, huxster, Castle street.

Maguire, Roger, blacksmith, Lower Water street.

Maguire, Mary, grocer and spirit-dealer, Water st.

Malcom, Rev. A. G. Upper Bridge street.

Mallon, Michael, butcher, Boat street.

Malone, Mary, huxster, Mill street.

Marlow, John, rope-maker, Mill street.

Marren, Dennis, stonecutter, High street.

Marshall, John, grocer and spirit-dealer, Market street.

Marshall, Joseph, haberdasher, Market street.

Marshall, Esther, haberdasher, North street.

Marshall, Ralph, turner, Hill street.

Martin, Andrew, gardener, Turner hill.

Mason, George, agent, coach-office, Margaret sq.

Mason, Jane, huxster, Needham street.

Matchet, Richard, carpenter, Canal street.

Mathews, Thomas, publican, *Ship*, Castle street.

Maunsell, Nicholas, district paymaster, Basin.

May, James, marble manufacturer, Dublin bridge.

Maynes, Miles, huxster, North street.

Maxwell, Letitia, Boat street.

Mee, Jane, haberdasher, North street.

Melling, John, merchant, Needham place.

Miller, George, surgeon and apothecary, Market st.

Milligan, Edward, carrier, Lower Water street.

Millikin, Samuel, wheelwright, Boat street.

Mines, Rev. Terence, Monaghan street.

Mines, James, mason, Queen street.

Minnitt, Robert M. capt. Monaghan militia, Boat street.

Mitchell, Joseph, publican, *Fox and Goose*, Sugar island.

Mitchell, George, shoemaker, Canal street.

Mitchell, Anne, Canal street.

Mitchell, Thomas, printer, Boat street.

Mitchell, Elizabeth, silkdier, Boat street.

Mitchell, William, painter and glazier, Boat street.

Mollan, John, apothecary, Market street.

Mollan, James, butter inspector, Canal street.

Monaghan John, mason, Catherine lane.

Monteith, Sarah, Castle street.

Mooney, John, clothes-dealer, North street.

Moore, James, post-master, Hill street.

Moore, James, printer, North street.

Moore, Margaret, Canal street.

Moore, Christopher, surveyor of excise, Needham place.

Moore, Patrick, currier, Boat street.

Moore, William, nailer, High street.

Moore, Thomas, nailer, North street.

Moore, A. H. huxter, Boat street.

Morgan, James, accountant, Kildare street.

Morgan, — dress-maker, Kildare street.

Morgan, Thomas, butcher, Bridge street.

Morgan, Edward, publican, Mill street.

Morgan, John, blue-dier, William street.

Morgan, Rosanna, confectioner, Water street.

Morgan, Francis, publican, Bridge street.

Morgan, James, shoemaker, Canal street.

Morrison, John, M. D. Needham place.

Mulligan, James, gent. Canal street.

Munns, Benjamin, stone-cutter, High street.

Murphy, Lawrence, sen. gent. Market street.
Murphy, Lawrence, jun. tanner, Downshire road.
Murphy, William, huxter, High street.
Murphy, Henry, journeyman chandler, Kiln Yard.
Murphy, Patrick, saddler & harness-maker, Hill st.
Murphy, Joseph, spirit-dealer, King street.
Murphy, Patrick, slater, Boat street.
Murray, William, waiter, Lower Water street.
Murtaugh, Anne, tallow chandler, Castle street.

M^c

M'Adam, Owen, tallow chandler, High street.
M'Aleavy, Christopher, taylor, Boat street.
M'Allister, James, huxter, Water street.
M'Alinden, James, baker, North street.
M'Anulty, John, Boat street.
M'Avoy, Mark, warehouseman, Monaghan street.
M'Avoy, Thomas, carpenter, Boat street.
M'Avoy, Richard, carpenter, Stream street.
M'Blain, David, accountant, Mill street.
M'Burney, James, schoolmaster, Market street.
M'Calpin, George, publican, *Ship,* King street.
M'Calpin, William, publican, Kiln street.
M'Camley, Sarah, Bridge street.
M'Camley, Henry, grocer and spirit-dealer, Castle street.
M'Camley, John, grocer and spirit-dealer, Castle st.
M'Camley, Patrick, merchant, Canal street.
M'Camley, John, hair-dresser, Water street.
M'Camley, Terence, publican, *Harp and Crown,* North street.
M'Camley, Bridget, publican, North street.
M'Cammon, Joseph, smith & farrier, Lower Water street.
M'Cann, William, eating-house, Merchants' quay.
M'Cann, Robert, clerk in distillery, Monaghan st.

M'Cann, Bridget, delf and china warehouse, North street.
M'Cann, Francis, wholesale & retail grocer, North street.
M'Cann, Bernard, dealer in marine stores, Market street.
M'Cardell, Owen, hostler, Canal street.
M'Cardell, Henry, cooper, Mill street.
M'Cardell, Daniel, rope-maker, High street.
M'Cartney, Mary Ann, Dromalane.
M'Clenahan, James, merchant, Merchants' quay.
M'Clements, George, rope-maker, Stream street.
M'Clune, George, printer, Boat street.
M'Convill, Matthew, tailor, Kiln street.
M'Convill, Ann, publican, North street.
M'Convill, Hugh, huxster, Castle street,
M'Conway, James, surveyor and gauger, King st.
M'Conwell, Anthony, tailor, Market street.
M'Cormick, Edward, schoolmaster, Boat street.
M'Cormick, Arthur, publican, Castle street.
M'Cormick, Thomas, tanner, Hide market.
M'Corry, Henry, hardware dealer, North street.
M'Court, John, clothes-dealer, North street.
M'Court, Ellen, publican, Canal street.
M'Coy, Matthew, tanner, Marcus square.
M'Cracken, Robert, book-keeper, Dromalane.
M'Crudden, Hugh, flaxdresser, Boat street.
M'Crum, Robert, clothes-dealer, North street.
M'Cullough, Robert, salemaster, King street.
M'Cune, Robert, professor of music, New street.
M'Dermott, William, plowmaker, High street.
M'Dine, William, baker, Boat street.
M'Donald, James, schoolmaster, Canal street.
M'Donald, Nicholas, sawyer, Canal street.
M'Donald, Eliza, dressmaker, Market street.
M'Donald, William, painter and glazier, North st.

M'Donald, — tailor, Water street.

M'Dowell, William, Welsh hotel, Canal street.

M'Farlin, Owen, huxter, Castle street.

M'Gahan, Hugh, carrier, Boat street.

M'Givern, John, butter and cattle-dealer, Mill st.

M'Glathery, William, grocer, High street.

M'Gowan, Patrick, nailer, Boat street.

M'Gowan, Geo. publican, *General Wolfe,* North st.

M'Gowan, Samuel, tidewaiter, Boat street.

M'Gowan, John, farmer, Boat street.

M'Gowan, Robert, tidewaiter, Boat street.

M'Gowan, John, nailer, Boat street.

M'Grath, Thomas, whitesmith, Sugar island.

M'Grath, Luke, whitesmith, Sugar island.

M'Grath, Lawrence, carpenter, William street.

M'Grath, Richard, coppersmith, Water street.

M'Grath, William, butcher, Castle street.

M'Grath, Robert, shoemaker, High street.

M'Guffin, Richard, shoemaker. Church street.

M'Guffin, Hugh, shoemaker, Church street.

M'Guffin, Robert, tobacco-spinner. Church street.

M'Henry, Charles, bluedier, North street.

M'Kavett, Moses, carpenter, carman's inn, Bridge st.

M'Kay, David, weaver, Queen street.

M'Kay, Henry, book agent, North street.

M'Kenna, John, eating house, Water street.

M'Kenna, Terence, brewer and malster, Queen st.

M'Kenna, William, baker, Hide street.

M'Keown. James, shoemaker, Market street.

M'Keown, Felix, schoolmaster, Monaghan street.

M'Keown, James, whitesmith, North street.

M'Kenny, John, bookseller and stationer, manufacturer of portable blacking, &c. Market st.

M'Kinley, George, sawyer, Boat street.

M'Kinley, Henry, sawyer, Boat street.

M'Kinley, James, blacksmith, Boat street.

M'Kitrick, James, boot and shoemaker, Hill-street.

M'Linn, Margaret, staymaker, Sugar island.

M'Mahon, Thomas, stonecutter, William street.

M'Mahon, Patrick, reedmaker, Kiln yard.

M'Manus, Daniel, baker, Mill street.

M'Manus, Elinor, clothes-dealer, North street.

M'Meaken, Robert, ship-broker and auctioneer, Canal
    street; office, Sugar island.

M'Minn, Joseph, soap-boiler and tallow chandler, Sugar island.

M'Mullen, Alexander, millwright, Boat street.

M'Naghten & Dalzel, tobacconists, grocers, spirit-dealers,
    and soap and candle manufacturers, North street.

M'Nally, Bernard, baker, Lower Water street.

M'Namara, Patrick, noggin-maker, North-street.

M'Namara, John, noggin-maker, North street.

M'Neill, Hector, warehouseman, Canal street.

M'Neill, Robert, classical school, Hill street.

M'Parlin, Daniel, shoemaker, Lower Water street.

M'Quillin, William, sawyer, church street.

M'Shane, Nicholas, cartmaker, Mill street.

M'Sherry, Edward, publican, *Duke of Wellington,* North
    street.

M'Vey, Mary, commercial coffee-room, Hill street.

M'Waters, — huxter, Kiln street.

N

NEAL, Peter, cooper, Needham place.

Nelson, John, printer, Lower Water street.

Nelson, Margaret, manufacturer of Prussian blue paper, for
    linen-drapers, &c. Lower Water st.

Nesbitt, Joseph, butter merchant, Merchants' quay.
Nesbitt, Harriet, haberdasher, Hill street.
Nevil, Henry, chairmaker, Pound street.
Nicholson, John, cooper, Queen street.
Nicholson, James, shoemaker, Canal street.
Nicholson, William, cooper, Lower Water street.
Nugent, James, haberdasher, North street.

O

O'BRIEN, Cornelius, leather-cutter, Mill street.
O'Byrne, Frances, seminary for young ladies, Edward street.
O'Byrne, John, eating-house, Canal street.
O'Donnell, John, chapman, Canal street.
O'Donnell, William, blackball manufacturer, Water street.
O'Donnell, Michael, clothes-dealer, North street.
Ogle, John, attorney, Canal street.
Ogle, Hans, gent. Dromalane.
Ogle, George, attorney, Hill street.
Ogle, William, Turner hill.
Ogle, Samuel, notary public and master of chancery, Hill street.
O'Hagan, John, woollen-draper, Market street.
O'Hagan, Arthur, woollen-draper, North street.
O'Hagan, Mary, woollen-draper, Market street.
O'Hanlon, — Monaghan street.
O'Hanlon, C. & M. haberdashers, North street.
O'Hanlon, Mary, huxster, Mill street.
O'Hanlon, Patrick, barrister at law, Hill street.
O'Hare, Michael, spirit-dealer, Boat street.
O'Hare, Michael, wheelwright, Boat street.
O'Hare, James, baker, Boat street.
O'Hare, Hugh, broguemaker, Boat street.
O'Hare, Hugh, baker, Courtney hill.

O'Neill, John, cooper, Mill street.
O'Neill, Francis, lodging-house, Water street.
O'Neill, James, farmer, High street.
O'Rourke, Peter, haberdasher, North street.
Orr, John, merchant, Canal street.
Osborne, William, confectioner, Hill street.

P

PARKS, John, accountant, Catherine street.
Parker, James, nailer, High street.
Parsons, Samuel, flour merchant, Trevor hill.
Patterson, John, shoemaker, Boat street.
Pattison, Wm. brazier and tin plate worker, Margaret street.
Pattison, John, sawyer, Church street.
Peacock, Alexander, Trevor hill.
Peden, Thomas, linen draper and hosier, Hill st.
Pepper, John, gent. Hill street.
Peterson, Francis, gunsmith and beam maker, Mill street.
Pike, William, shoemaker, Canal street.
Pix, Corbett, shoemaker, King street.
Pockridge, Michael, painter and glazier, Kiln st.
Polin, Thomas, publican, Castle street.
Pooler, Robert, merchant, Canal street.
Power, John, leather-cutter, North street.
Prentice, James, public notary and commissioner for taking
    affidavits, Market street.
Pugh, Captain, Queen street.
Purdon, Robert, merchant and ship-broker, Merchants'
    quay.

Q

QUINN, John, merchant, Kildare street.
Quinn, Mrs. Henry, Canal street.

Quinn, George, clothes dealer, North street.

Quinn, Charles, huxster, Boat street.

Quinn, John, nailer, High street.

Quinn, James, nailer, North street.

Quin, Patrick & James, grocers, spirit-dealers and bakers, Kildare street.

Quin, Bernard, saddler, Canal street.

Quin, Ann, dealer in earthenware, North street.

Quin, Luke, grocer and spirit merchant, North st.

R

Rankin, Edward, linen bleacher and cotton spinner, Canal street.

Ravenhill, Courtney, butter merchant, Canal st.

Raverty, Terence, clothes-dealer, North street.

Reid, Samuel, distributer of stamps, Canal street.

Reid, Samuel, jun. attorney, Canal street.

Reid, James, shoemaker, William street.

Reid, James, sawyer, Pound street.

Reid, Matthew, joiner and builder, Stream street.

Reilly, James, salt merchant, Castle street.

Reilly, Thomas, coachmaker, Lower Water street.

Remage, M. huxter, Canal street.

Revel, James, publican, *Cock,* North street.

Reynold, Thomas, shoemaker, Canal street.

Rice, Thomas, sawyer, High street.

Rice, John, shoemaker, High street.

Rice, Terence, schoolmaster, Market street.

Rice, Ann, grocer, chandler and tobacco manufacturer, Market street.

Rice, Henry, dealer, Mill street.

Rick, Mary, Hill street.

Riddle, James, carpenter, Church street.

Riggs, George, carpenter, High street.

Robinson, William, hawker, Boat street.

Robinson, William, carman's inn, Canal street.

Robinson, William, carpenter, Canal street.

Rogers, George, breeches maker and glover, Margaret square.

Rooney, Hugh, blacksmith, Queen street.

Rooney, Bernard, blacksmith, William street.

Rooney, Charles, haberdasher, North street.

Rooney, Peter, cooper, New street,

Rooney, Hugh, bluedier, Boat street.

Rooney, Mary, bluedier, Castle street.

Rooney, William, carpenter, Castle lane.

Ross, Christopher, leather-cutter and bellows manufacturer, North street.

Rowan, Robert Ross, William street.

Rowan, Alexander, printer, Water street.

Rowan, John, shoemaker, High street.

Ruddle, William, painter and glazier, North street.

Ruddy, Thomas, carrier, Pound street.

Ruddy, Patrick, cartmaker, Needham street.

Russell, John, attorney, Boat street.

Russell, Matthew, rope & sail-maker, Sugar island.

Russell, Miles, baker, Sugar island.

Russell, Robert, coachmaker, Hill street.

Russell, M'Kenna & Co. brewers, Queen street.

Ryan, Lawrence, grocer and spirit-dealer, Boat st.

Ryan, James, publican, High street.

Ryan, Daniel, stuccoman and plasterer, High st.

Ryan, James, carpenter, Pound street.

Ryan, John, ropemaker, Pound street.

Ryan, William, carpenter, Queen street.

S

SALMON, Ephraim, accountant, Canal street.

Sands, Michael, huxter, Boat street.

Savage, John, wholesale grocer, tobacco, soap and candle manufacturer, Sugar island.

Savage, Edward T. surveyor of excise, High street.

Savage, John, auctioneer, High street.

Savage, Jane, dealer in glass & earthenware, North street.

Savage, Henry, grocer, spirit-dealer and tobacco manufacturer, North street.

Savage, William, grocer, North street.

Scott, George, grocery and gunpowder warehouse, Market street.

Scott, Michael, stonecutter, Boat street.

Scott, William, gardener, Canal street.

Scott & Nelson, wholesale and retail grocers, Sugar island.

Scott, David, wholesale grocer, Water street.

Searight, James, woollen-draper, Market street.

Searight, James, woollen-draper, North street.

Seeds, Thomas, captain of St. Patrick, Mill street.

Serjeson, John, shoemaker, High street.

Sharkey, Robert, merchant, Edward street.

Sharkey, Patrick, iron and brass-founder, Edward street.

Sharkey, Peter, boot & shoemaker, Needham street.

Sharkey, Dominick, grocer, Mill street.

Shaw, Wm. agent at the mail coach office; house, William street.

Shedwick, George, wood turner, King street.

Shields, Thomas, gent. Edward st. Corry square.

Shields, Richard, carpenter, Queen street.

Sheill, Charles C. revenue officer, Boat street.

Shehan, Robert, pro-collector, Boat street.

Sheeran, Thomas, butcher, High street.
Sherry, Thomas, publican, *George and Dragon.*
Short, John, tidewaiter, North street.
Short, Alexander, North street.
Shoulder, Arthur, publican, North street.
Simple, John, sawyer, Pound street.
Simpson, Ebenezer, currier and tanner, Old quay.
Skeffington, Hugh, tanner, Boat street.
Sloan, Nicholas, gent. Monaghan street.
Sloan, James, book-keeper, King street.
Sloan, John, tailor, Mill street.
Small, Hugh, leather merchant, Castle street.
Small, John, grocer and spirit-dealer, Margaret st.
Small, Hugh, publican, High street.
Smith, John, cabinet-maker, William street.
Smith, Isaac, cabinet maker, Kildare street.
Smith, John, shoemaker, North street.
Smith, Philip, dealer, Market street.
Smith, Bridget, grocer, Boat street.
Smith, Henry, book-keeper, Catherine lane, Canal st.
Spence, Thomas, grocer and spirit dealer, Canal st.
Spence & Moore, wholesale grocers, Canal-street.
Spencer, John, hairdresser, Water street.
Spotswood, Henry, saddler, Boat street.
Spotswood, George, saddler, Courtney hill.
Stephenson, Rev. George, William street.
Stevenson, James, bookseller and stationer, North street.
Stewart, A. & J. haberdashers, North street.
Stewart, George, gent. Boat street.
Story, Benjamin, grocer and gardener, Barrack st.
Stuart, James, gent. Bridge street.
Swanzy and Wilson, merchants, Sugar-house quay.

T

TAGGART, Owen, grocer, Market street.
Taylor, Robert, apothecary, Boat street.
Templeton, Thomas, boot and shoemaker, North street.
Templeton, Mrs. Catherine, Hill street.
Thom, Mrs. Trevor hill.
Thompson, Robert, distiller, Monaghan street.
Thompson, William, foundryman, Monaghan st.
Thompson, John, bridewell-keeper, Ballybot.
Thompson, Robert, publican, *Ship*, King street.
Thompson, Henry, wine and spirit merchant, Sugar island.
Thompson, James, publican, *Ship*, North street.
Thompson, Nicholas, cutler, North street.
Thompson, Mrs. Hanna, Trevor hill.
Thompson, George, bridewell keeper, Castle st.
Thompson, Archibald, publican, Boat street.
Thompson, John, sawyer, Church street.
Thompson, William, wheelwright, High street.
Thompson, Hugh, tailor, Boat street.
Thompson, John, hat warehouse, North street.
Thompson, William, shoemaker, Church street.
Tierney, Hugh, cutler, Boat street.
Todd, John, grocer, soap-boiler and tallow chandler, North
    street.
Tosh, Wm. grocer and spirit-dealer, Sugar island.
Towers, William, coachmaker, Queen street.
Townley, Samuel & James, merchants, Merchants' quay.
Townley, John, shopkeeper, Market street.
Toy, John, nailer, North street.
Treanor, John, publican, Canal street.
Treanor, Pat. hotel and tavern, *New White Cross,* Margaret
    street.

Treanor, Owen, broguemaker, Lower Water st.
Treanor, Terence, haberdasher and linen-draper, North
    street.
Tronson, Lawford, gent. Hill street.
Turley, Daniel, blacksmith, Hill street.
Turley, Patrick, haberdasher & linen-draper, North street.
Turley, Henry, grocer, High street.

V

VERDON, Thomas, M. D. Market street.
Verdon, Michael, apothecary, Castle street.

W

WADE, William, printer, William street.
Wade, Eliza, dress-maker, William street.
Wallace, Robert, pro-collector of excise, Canal street.
Wallace, J. H. wine merchant, Kildare street; house, Basin.
Wallace, Andrew, surveyor of excise, Kildare st.
Wallace, Samuel, wine merchant, Hill street.
Walker, Isaac, wine merchant, Canal street.
Walsh, Richard, woollen-draper, agent to the Atlas
    Insurance, Market street.
Waring, Thomas, Esq. Trevor hill.
Waring, David, hackle-maker, Boat street.
Webb, William, master of Lancasterian school, Boat street.
Webb, — teacher of the piano forte, Barrack st.
Wheley, Capt John, Bridge street.
White, Mary, huxter, Queen street.
White, David & Henry, merchants, Canal quay.
White, Michael, carpenter, High street.
White, David, merchant; house, Boat street.
White, John, hardware merchant and ironmonger, North street.

Whitehead, Richard, pawnbroker, Boat street.

Wickston, Samuel, shuttle-maker, Castle street.

Wier, William, shoemaker, North street.

Willis, Mrs. Elizabeth, Dromalane.

Wilkinson, Alexander, printer and publisher of the *Newry Commercial Telegraph*, bookseller, stationer, and patent medicine vender, Margaret square.

Wilson, James, land surveyor, Canal street.

Wilson, William, brick-maker, King street.

Wilson, John, shoemaker, North street.

Wilson, James, soap-boiler, High street.

Wiseman, James, cabinet-maker, Church street.

Withers, James, publican, Mill street.

Woods, John, surgeon & apothecary, Sugar island.

Woods, George, gardener, Courtney hill.

Wright, Joseph, gent. Hill street.

Y

Young, Mary C. haberdasher, Castle street.

Historical Account of Warrenpoint and Rosstrevor

At about a mile from the end of Newry, is Greenwood Park, the property of Ross Thompson, jun. Esq. The view of Fathom, on the opposite side, is extremely fine. Green Island is the next object that meets the eye, where there are very ancient salt-works, the property of Mr. Hugh Campbell. After passing this place, the observer may perceive, within the compass of five hundred yards, two provinces, Ulster and Leinster, and three counties, Down, Armagh and Louth.

Approaching nearer to Mount-hall, the prospect exhibits a picturesque view of Narrow-water castle and ferry. This castle was built by the Duke of Ormond, and has been converted into a salt-work, at present the property of Messrs. St. Lawrence Smyth and Co.

Warrenpoint is, comparatively speaking, a new village. About sixty years ago, it had only one house, which stood near the sea-shore, at a distance from the road, and which belonged to Mr. Christopher Aiken. At present it has a very considerable number, and is improving every year. There are many very comfortable lodging-houses in and around the village. The quay is very convenient, and is capable of receiving vessels of large burden. The wind-mill, built by Mr. Robert Turner, is a very valuable concern; the machinery, (a large proportion of which is of cast metal,) having been constructed on the most approved plan.

There was originally a very extensive rabbit-warren at Warrenpoint, from which circumstance the village has received its name.

Near the village stands the new Presbyterian meeting-house, lately erected on the site of the old one, on a very convenient plan.

On passing through Warrenpoint towards the shore, the prospect becomes extremely beautiful and grand. The bay, expanding to the view, forms a noble basin, where a thousand ships may ride in perfect safety, bounded on the right and left by the lofty, over-hanging mountain of Carlingford, whose base magnificently cuts the water, in a straight line of great extent, and by the finely-wooded mountain of Rosstrevor. In the horizon, the light-house and block-house, and the vessels passing the bar, present to the eye a very pleasing termination to the prospect.

Immediately to the right, and on the other side of the water, at Omeath, an elegant house, in the cottage style, lately built by James Bell, Esq. appears in view.

At Seaview, there is a row of neat houses, well situated for the accommodation of bathers. The prospects from this place, and from thence round to the quay of Rosstrevor, is extremely fine. The former place commands a view of the whole bay, the quay of Rosstrevor, and the adjoining wood, together with the entire vale, diversified with beautiful plantations, elegant cottages, and magnificent seats.

The seat of Francis Carleton, Esq. late collector of Newry, at present called Green Park, is pleasantly situated on the left hand, at a considerable distance from the road. The original house was built by James Moore, Esq. father of Christopher Moore, Esq. of Newry. It was occupied for a time, first by Mr. Strong, and afterwards by Mr. Broomfield. Collector Carleton having added an entire new front, has made the house a very fine mansion. The adjoining grounds have been laid out with very good taste.

The village of Rosstrevor is situated at the north-east extremity of the bay of Carlingford, at the foot of that extensive range of mountains which stretches along the shores of Mourne. It was anciently the seat of the Trevor family, and is admirably suited as a residence for persons in delicate health.

The building now occupied as a barrack, was erected by the

father of C. Moore, Esq. Major Ross having purchased the concern, added wings to it, and made it his place of residence.

A little further up the hill, stands the Roman Catholic chapel, a neat house, built about twenty years ago, but lately very much improved by the Rev. Mr. Gilmour.

At the upper end of the village, there is a very neat schoolhouse, lately built by Mrs. Dawson and Miss Balfour, who have established a school for the education of female children, twenty of whom receive instruction, gratis.

At about half a mile from the village, stand the ruins of the old church of Kilbroney. There is an ancient stone cross at this place, which is regarded by the peasantry with peculiar veneration. At a little distance there is a well also, at the foot of a gigantic ash, which is resorted to by great multitudes of persons, on particular occasions. Many families in the vicinity, continue to bury their dead within and around the ruins.

Kilbroney is the residence of Robert Martin, Esq. whose house commands a pleasant view of the extensive vale below, of part of the bay, and of the mountain of Carlingford. Mr. Martin has bleach-mills at this place, which are well situated, and supplied with an excellent head of water.

A little lower down is Mr. Black's paper-mill and dwelling-house. They were originally built by John Darley, Esq. and intended as an establishment for the bleaching of linen cloth.

At the quay are considerable salt-works, now wrought by Mr. James Reilly. The quay was formed, about seventy-five years ago by Mr. John Martin, whose name was engraved on a stone built into the wall of the pier, but the characters are now effaced.

On the shelving bank beneath the road, stands the Woodhouse, the residence of the Hon. and Rev. Edmund Knox, Dean of Down. The grounds are tastefully adorned with a great variety of trees and shrubs, suited to the situation, which, in the season, appear in great beauty and perfection.

After having passed from under the waving canopy of spreading oak, and ascended a gentle eminence, the bay once more presents its spreading bosom to the spectator's eye. To the right, Warrenpoint and the beautiful seats between Seaview and Rosstrevor, form a very charming prospect, while on the left is seen (finely contrasted) a tremendous, precipice of the adjoining mountain, "rude, barren, and bare." No words can paint the splendour of the scene, viewed in a calm summer evening, when all the varied glow that invests the western sky, and all the tints which surround the setting sun, purple, gold, and blue, are pictured on the unruffled bosom of the bay.

A very delightful scene is also exhibited from the shore at Seaview, in the fine evenings in summer and autumn, when the full moon, rising over the bay, in tranquil majesty, sheds a stream of light along the watery way.

The bay, almost encircled by mountains or high hills, has something the appearance of a vast amphitheatre, where the boats and ships, passing through the illumined expanse, are contemplated by the light of the lunar lamp, whose beams are beautifully reflected from the trembling waters.

The massive ruins of Greencastle stand upon a gut or inlet of the sea, a few miles below Rosstrevor. This castle was fortified by the Burghs, Earls of Ulster, and Lords of Connaught, and was reputed in ancient times, a place of considerable strength. It was rendered famous by two marriages of illustrious persons, which were celebrated within its walls, in 1312—one of Maurice Fitz-Thomas and Catherine, daughter to the Earl of Ulster, and the other of Thomas Fitz-John, and another daughter of the same nobleman. It was destroyed by the Irish in 1343, but was soon after repaired and rendered stronger than before. It appears by a record of the first of Henry IV. that both Greencastle and the castle of Carlingford were governed by one constable, the better to secure a communication between the English settlers in the counties of Louth and Down. Stephen Gernon was constable of both castles at that time, and had a yearly salary of £20 for Greencastle, and £5 for Carlingford. About the end of the 15th century, it was considered to be of so much importance to the crown that none but Englishmen by birth were eligible to the office of constable. It had a garrison in the rebellion of 1641, which served to check the progress of the insurgents in the adjacent districts. It appears from ancient records, that it had been the residence of the Bagnal family at an early period.

Rosstrevor has improved very much of late years, and contains at present several handsome houses. Topsyturvy, built by William Maguire, Esq. naturally attracts the observation of strangers, from the singularity of its appearance. It stands on the side of a steep hill, from which there is a pleasant prospect. There is no uniformity whatever in the building; and the kitchen is situated in the upper story. Mrs. Dawson, relict of the late Dean Dawson, a few years ago, erected a house on a very novel plan, which, from its situation, promises to be a charming residence. Mr. Martin has also lately built a very good house in the street leading to the quay. Admiral Fortescue's house, built by Mrs. Maguire, stands in a most delightful situation. Smithson Corry, Esq. has lately fitted up a lodge in a very elegant style. Captain Wright and others have also added, by their improvements, to the beauty of the place.

A handsome church has lately been erected in Rosstrevor, which has contributed much to the beautiful appearance of the village.

On the 26th of January, 1819, a Savings Bank was instituted in Warrenpoint, for the purpose of affording to the industrious poor, a safe place of deposit for their savings. The office is open every Tuesday from 12 till 3 o'clock in the afternoon. Sums so low as 10d. at one time, and not exceeding £50 in one year, will be received from any individual. The Marquis of Downshire is patron of the institution. The vice patrons are—the Earl of Annesley, Viscount Killmorey, Viscount Glerawley, the Bishop of Dromore, and the Bishop of Down. There are nine trustees, a treasurer, and a committee, composed of eighteen of the most respectable gentlemen in the neighbourhood, who meet at stated times, to inspect the accounts and regulate the business of the institution.

Directory of Warrenpoint, for 1819.

A

Adderley, Alexander, surgeon.
Alcorn, John, publican.
Arnold, Rev. Samuel.

B

Bailie, Mrs. lodging-house.
Ballentine, Robert, tidewaiter.
Barry, Samuel, ship-carpenter.
Brewer, R. tidewaiter.
Bryden, Miss, grocer and lodging-house.
Burns, Patrick, pilot.
Burns, Hugh, lodging-house.

C

Campbell, J. schoolmaster.
Carlile, H. tidewaiter.
Carter, Samuel, tidewaiter.
Catilly, Martin, coal-porter.
Cautry, D. attorney.
Clinton, William, butcher.
Cooly, James, publican.
Connolly, James, publican.
Connolly, Stephen, blacksmith.
Cord, William, captain.

Creek, Edward, gent. *Narrow-water.*
Creighton, Robert, schoolmaster.
Cummins, Samuel, lodging-house.
Cunningham, Hugh, publican.
Cunningham, Andrew, shoemaker.
Curran, Hugh, publican.

D

DAVIS, Rev. John, rector.
Davis, George, grocer.
Davis, William, lodging-house and delf shop.
Dixon, Mrs. lodging-house.
Dogherty, Daniel, publican and chandler.
Douglass, Mrs.
Donaven, Miss, grocer and lodging-house.
Dunbar, Mrs. lodging-house.

E

EARL, James, publican.

F

FERRAN, James, marriner.
Ferran, Patrick, ship-carpenter.
Finnigan, William, publican.
Fivey, Mr.
Fitzgerald, Richard, boatman.
Flanagan, Miss, lodging-house.
Forest, Mrs. post-mistress.
Forest, William, lodging-house.
Forest, William, captain.
Fullerton, Mr. lodging-house.

G

GATES, Sarah, grocer and lodging-house.
Gossan, John, publican.
Glenny, George, brewer.
Goodwin, Richard, captain and lodging-house.
Gray, John, farmer and lodging-house.

H

HATAN, James, captain.
Hagan, Matthew, tailor and lodging-house.
Hall, Roger, Esq. *Narrow-water.*
Hamilton, John, ship-carpenter.
Hamilton, James, boatman.
Harrison, James, coal-factor.
Henry, William, excise officer.
Hennan, Absalom, grocer and lodging-house.
Hollywood, Hall, lodging-house.

I

IRWIN, Thomas, surgeon.
Irwin, John, gent.

J

JIGGS, James, lodging-house.

K

KINKADE, James, publican.
Kinny, Patrick, publican.

L

LAVERY, Richard, lodging-house.

Lawson, James, gent. *Narrow-water.*
Lawson, Thomas, tidewaiter.
Lundy, Thomas, boatman.
Levens, J. mariner.

M

MAGAN, Miss, school-mistress.
Magenny, Charles, nailer.
Magennis, Con. tidewaiter.
Magennety, Alexander, tidewaiter.
Magowan, M. grocer and lodging-house.
Maguire, H. tidewaiter.
Major, Mrs. lodging-house.
Manier, Andrew, merchant, *Narrow-water.*
Maxwell, Mrs.
Morgan, William, mariner.
Montgomery, Hans, ship-carpenter.
Moody, Miss.
Mooney, Owen, blacksmith.
Moore, William, Esq.
Moore, Robert, carpenter.
Moore, Charles, Esq.
Morgan, John, carpenter.
Morrison, John, publican.
Mullen, Timothy, lodging-house.
Mullen, Bernard, publican.
Mullen, Peter, grocer and lodging-house.
Murney, Thomas, publican.
Murney, Mary.
Murphy, Ann, lodging-house.
Murray, Thomas, publican.

Mᶜ

M'Areavy, George, publican.
M'Bride, Robert, gent.
M'Cormick, Owen, blacksmith.
M'Cormick, R. carpenter.
M'Crumb, James, shoemaker.
M'Donnell, J. tailor and lodging-house.
M'Dermott, David, *Narrow-water.*
M'Dermott, Charles, miller, *Narrow-water.*
M'Neill, Archibald, shoemaker.
M'Veigh, Edward, publican.
M'Williams, George, lodging-house.

N

Neilis, John, boatman.
Nevin, Hugh, boatman.
Nevin, Mrs. Mary.

O

Overn, John, accountant.
Overn, William, porter-house.
Owen, John, lodging-house.

P

Patterson, Thomas, shoemaker.
Perry, Swift, gent.
Plunket, Edward, painter and glazier.
Polan, Rev. Mr. P. P.

R

Roche, Robert, broker, dock-master and interpreter.

S

Seeds, Samuel, grocer.
Sheriff, Peter, architect.
Shields, Mrs.
Shields, Isaac, ship-builder, *Green Island*.
Shields, Patrick, publican, *Green Island*.
Sims, Andrew, innkeeper.
Slater, William, revenue officer.
Smith, Joseph, musician.
Smyth & Craig, salt manufacturers, *Narrow-water*.

T

Taggart, Thomas, boatman.
Templeton, Patrick, lodging-house.
Thomboe, Michael, broker and linguist, *Narrow-water*.
Thompson, James lodging-house.
Tombes, Richard, acting admiral of Carlingford bay.
Turner, Robert, Esq.
Turner, Samuel, brewer.

W

Wade, Benjamin, druggist.
Wade, Mrs. lodging-house.
Wardlow, James, joiner.
Watson, John, deputy port-surveyor.
Wescot, Mrs. publican.
Wright, Watson, lodging-house.

Directory of Rosstrevor, for 1819.

B

Bagwell, Mrs. *Moygannon.*
Bagwell, Captain.
Balfour, Miss, *River side.*
Balfour, Mrs. *River side.*
Bell, Miss.
Bingham, John, M. D.
Black, Thomas, paper manufacturer.
Boyle, Mrs. publican and lodging-house, *Quay.*
Bradley, Daniel, slater and plasterer.
Branagan, Alexander, boatman, *Quay.*
Broom, Alexander, lodging-house.
Brownlow, Mrs. *Richmond.*
Byrne, Miss.

C

Carroll, Anthony, musician and lodging-house.
Carroll, Miss, dressmaker.
Carey, Michael, musician.
Caulfield, Roger, mason.
Cooley, Robert, papermaker.
Corry, Carlile, Esq.
Courtney, Captain, *Drumpark cottage.*
Courtney, Charles and Co.
Creighton, Mary, lodging-house.

Cunnan, James, whitesmith.
Cunningham, Thomas, publican.
Cunningham, James, nailer.

D

Dawson, Mrs. Vesy, *River side.*
Dean of Down, Hon. and Very Rev. *Wood-house.*
Devay, Miss, governess of Miss Balfour's school.
Dobson, William, linen-draper, *Linton lodge.*

E

Evans, Rev. J. T. vicar of *Kilbroney.*

F

Fegan, William, boatman, *Quay.*
Feran, Hugh, lodging-house.
Feran, John, huxter.
Feran, George, musician.
Feran, Matthew, butcher.
Flanagan, James, publican.
Fortescue, Sir Chichester, admiral, *Cregfield.*
Fortescue, Colonel, *Greghill.*
Fortescue, Mrs. senr. *Cregfield.*

G

Givesom, — gent. *Broom hedge.*
Gilmore, Rev. James, P. P.
Grandy, John, lodging-house.
Gray, Ephraim, tailor.
Gribbon, Patrick, blacksmith.

H

HANITY, Ellen, lodging-house.
Hart, John, joiner.
Hart, John, jun. joiner.
Hart, James, musician.
Hewitt, Hon. James.
Hill, Henry, mariner.
Hopkins, Richard, hair-dresser.

I

IRWIN, Mrs. dressmaker and lodging-house.

J

JACKSON, John, assistant deputy barrackmaster.
Jones, William, surgeon, royal navy.

K

KEAN, Daniel, revenue boatman.
Kelly, Peter, butcher.
Kerr, John, merchant.
Kerr, Mrs. Ann, grocer, spirit-dealer and lodging-house.
Kerr, Patrick, baker.
Kerr, Elinor, lodging house.
Kerr, Charles, blacksmith.
Knox, Right Hon. George.

L

LANE, William, shoemaker.
Law, Thomas, schoolmaster.
Lennon, John.
Lifford, Lord Viscount, *Arno's vale,*
Loughlan, John, lodging-house.

M

MARTIN, Margaret, grocer.
Martin, Robert, linen-draper, *Kilbroney.*
Moffet, John and Sons, sawyers.
Moore, Mrs. E.
Morgan, Hugh, grocer.
Morgan, Patrick, tailor.
Murphy, Patrick, shoemaker,

M^c

M'ALISTER, Daniel, haberdasher.
M'Cormick, John, blacksmith.
M'Cover, James, slater and plasterer.
M'Given, William, sen. Esq.
M'Given, William, jun. Esq.
M'Kain, Alexander, lodging-house.
M'Keown, Michael, cooper.
M'Levy, T. hawker.

N

NEILL, Rev. John, R. C. curate.
Newell, Francis, farmer, *Killowan.*
Newell, Robert, farmer, *Killowan.*
Nooney, Robert, jauntingcar-keeper.

Q

QUIN, Terence, farmer.

R

REED, Captain, *Belview.*
Reilly, James, merchant and salt-refiner.

Reilly, John Lushington, Esq.
Ross, Mrs. *Bladensburg.*
Ross, D. R. Esq. *Lodge.*
Ross, Edward, Esq. *Lodge.*
Ross, Mrs.
Ross, Thomas, shoemaker.
Ross, James, revenue boatman, *Quay.*
Ruxton, Richard, Esq. *Ballyedmond.*

S

Sarsfield, Mrs. subscription shop.
Saunderson, Mrs.
Savage, Jane, grocer.
Sharkey, Philip, blacksmith.
Sharkey, Henry, tidewaiter.
Sloan, John, mariner.
Small, James, linen merchant, *Killowan.*
Small, Joseph, farmer, *Killowan.*
Smith, Captain.
Spence, George, revenue boatman.
Spencer, Mrs. Catherine.
Stevenson, Richard, joiner.
Stewart, Alexander, *Ballyedmond.*
Stuart, Charles, postmaster.
Stuart, Robert, lodging-house.

T

Tempest, William, musician and lodging-house.
Thunder, Henry, gent.
Trainor, John, joiner.
Tumalty, William, shoemaker.

W

WARD, Edward, innkeeper.
Warring, Rev. Holt, *Rosetta.*
Willis, Robert, joiner and builder.
Wilson, Samuel, miller, *Millbank.*
Wilson, John, baker.
Wrey, Mrs.
Wright, Matthew, gent.

Y

YOUNG, Mrs.

Historical Account of Kilkeel and Mourne.

THE earliest account which can be given of the district of Mourne, is, that it was bestowed, in the twelfth century, to the abbey of Newry, on condition that a certain number of monks should reside among the inhabitants, to perform religious duties, teach schools, &c. A remarkable clause in this grant, states, that a certain portion of land should be cleared of timber, every year—an evident proof how thinly the country was inhabited at that period. Under Elizabeth, it was transferred from the original proprietors to Sir Henry Bagnal, and afterwards to his daughter, who married into the Nedham family. It now remains in the possession of Lord Viscount Kilmorey, to whose ancestor it was left by William Nedham, Esq.

Kilkeel, a handsome village, is situated near the sea, and distant from Rosstrevor, seven miles. A new church has lately been erected here, which adds much to the beauty of the place. There is a Dissenting meeting-house, attended by a most respectable congregation, and a Roman Catholic chapel is nearly completed, in the neighbourhood of the town.

The inhabitants of this place, and the surrounding country, are noted for their hospitality and attention to strangers. In the summer season, the shore might be made the resort of bathers and invalids, from the fine sandy beach which here presents itself to the eye; and were a few neat houses erected contiguous to it, there is not the least doubt of many visiters preferring it to its rival, Newcastle.—About three miles from Kilkeel, stands the light-house, a very fine building, one hundred and twenty feet in height. The light may be observed at the distance of ten leagues.—Annalong, a small village, situated on this coast, is principally the resort of fishing boats. The prospect from hence to Newcastle is remarkably fine. On the right, the Irish Channel, and, on a clear day, the Isle of Man, may be distinctly seen. On the left, rugged mountains rear their heads, the principal of which, Slieve Donard, is of a conical form, and far exceedeth the others in height.

DIRECTORY OF KILKEEL, FOR 1819.

A

ADDERLY, Alexander, surgeon.
Adderly, John, dealer.
Atkinson, John, gent.
Atkinson, Edward, wholesale and retail grocer.
Austin, James, grocer and wheelwright.

B

BEECH, Charles, *Killmorey house.*
Boyd, David, linen merchant.
Buchanan, carpenter, *Ballykeel.*
Byrne, Stephen, publican and grocer.

C

CAPSTON, Mrs. dressmaker and miliner.
Chesney, Alexander, Esq. surveyor, *Prospect.*
Corran, Felix, nailer.
Corran, Henry, nailer.
Cuming, Mary, publican.
Cuming. Edward, linen merchant, *Bullymagart* [sic].
Cuming, John, grocer.
Curar, Rev. Richard, P. P.

D

DAVIDSON, Robert, farmer, *Cranfield.*
Donnelson, William, baker.

Doran, Edward, tailor.
Dougherty, William, tallow-chandler.
Doyle, James, shoemaker and dealer.
Doyle, John, blue-dier.

E

EMERSON, William Clark, paper manufacturer.

F

FERAN, Owen, butcher.
Floyd, Stephen, publican.

G

GALAGHER, Bernard, paper-maker, *White River.*
Gibson, David, baker.
Gordon, Alexander, woollen-draper.
Graham, Thomas, surgeon.

H

HALLIDAY, Jane, grocer.
Halliday, Henry, farmer.
Hamilton, S. G. surgeon and apothecary.
Hamilton, Hugh, revenue officer, *Cranfield.*
Hamilton, James, grocer and leather-seller.
Hamilton, George, shoemaker.
Harrold, Daniel, smith and farrier.
Henderson, William, linen merchant, *Derryogue.*
Hill, Moses, mariner.
Hogan, Michael, paper-maker, *White River.*

I

IRWIN, James, linen merchant, *Dunavin.*

K

KIERNAN, Francis, butcher.
Killmorey, Right Hon. Viscount, *Killmorey house.*
Kinlar, John, dealer.

L

LAPPIN, Owen, paper-maker, *White River.*
Lewis, George, postmaster.

M

MARMION, Christopher, Esq. *Drumaron.*
Marmion, Arthur, spirit merchant.
Marmion, James, Esq. *Janebrook.*
Matthews, Mrs. Col. *Loyalty Farm.*
Mather, Samuel, grocer and publican.
Moore, David, Esq. *Shannon Grove.*
Moore, Nathaniel, innkeeper.
Moore, James, farmer, *Cranfield.*
Moore, James, publican.
Moore, William, Esq.
Moore, John, Esq. seneschal, *Moore Lodge.*
Moore, Charles, *Ballyvay.*
Moore, James, officer of customs.
Moore, James, farmer, *Ballymagough.*
Moore, David, farmer, *Benagh.*
Moore, William, *Ballynahattin.*
Murney, James, officer of excise.
Murphy, Richard, innkeeper.

Mc

M'Connell, James, painter and glazier.
M'Cullough, Bernard, publican.
M'Cullough, Bernard, paper-maker, *White River.*
M'Gravy, Rev. John.
M'Hassan, Mark, soap-boiler and tallow chandler.
M'Ilroy, Mrs. *Greencastle.*
M'Ilwain, Rev. John, *Cranfield.*
M'Night, Andrew, linen-draper & bleacher, *Greenfield.*
M'Neilly, Henry, Esq. *Moneydaragh.*
M'Neilly, Henry, Esq. *Mullertown.*
M'Neilly, James, Esq. *Glassdrummond.*
M'Neilly, Richard, Esq. *Moneydaragh.*
M'Neilly, George, Esq. *Moneydaragh.*

N

Nicholson, Joseph, farmer.
Nugent, Robert, shoemaker.

R

Richardson, Christopher, *Ballymagart.*
Rogers, Hugh, publican.

S

Seeds, Hugh, farmer.
Shannon, John, farmer, *Maghery.*
Shannon, William, farmer, *Maghery.*
Sibbett, James, linen manufacturer.
Sloan, William, grocer and woollen-draper.
Sloan, Richard, farmer, *Mourne Park.*
Sloan, Patrick, publican.

Sloan. Murtaugh, nailer.
Small, Mrs. Frances, farmer, *Cranfield,*
Small, John, farmer, *White River.*
Smith, John, farmer, *Mullertown.*
Smith, James, publican.
Smith, Patrick, carpenter.
Smith, William, shoemaker.
Stevenson, John, grocer.
Stevenson, Misses.

T

THOMPSON, John, gent.
Thompson, Robert, *Drumandoney.*
Twible, James, *Drumandoney.*
Twible, James, farmer, *Drumandoney.*

V

VAUGHAN, Arthur, baker.

W

WALMSLEY, John, farmer, *Derryogue.*
Walmsley, John, linen-draper and bleacher, *Ballykeel.*
Waring, Rev. Lucas, rector of Kilkeel.
Waring, John, Esq. *Bell hill.*
West, Peter, surveyor.
White, James, dealer.
Williamson, Andrew, clock and watchmaker.
Williamson, Andrew, haberdasher.
Wilson, John, farmer, *Ballymagough.*
Wisdom, William, shoemaker.
Wright, John, publican.

DIRECTORY OF RATHFRILAND, FOR 1819.

THE town of Rathfriland is agreeably situated on a large hill, and is a very pleasant village. It has one church—one Presbyterian meeting-house—one of Seceders—one of Covenanters—one of Quakers, and a congregation of Methodists. There is a very considerable weekly market held in Rathfriland, and also a very prosperous and well-attended Sunday-school, which promises to be of great advantage to the rising generation.

A

ADAMS, Gilbert, woollen-draper.
Adams, James, dealer.
Alexander, William and John, surgeons and apothecaries.
Alexander, Thomas, grocer.
Anderson, Marmaduke, surgeon.
Armour, William, publican.

B

BANNON, Patrick, publican.
Bannon, Charles, dealer.
Barber, Elizabeth, *Tullyqui.*
Beckett, James, earthenware dealer.
Bell, James, surgeon.
Bell, Edward, dealer.
Bell, J. and D. publicans.
Bell, Daniel, saddler.
Bell, John, carpenter.

Bennet, John, blacksmith.
Biers, Mrs. Ann.
Bowles, Adam, baker.
Boyd, John, cloth-lapper.
Boyle, — surgeon.
Boyle, John, grocer.
Bradford, Robert, clock and watchmaker.
Bradford, John, wheelwright.
Brice, Samuel, hatter.
Bullock, Ezekiel, wheelwright.
Burns, Hugh, blacksmith.
Byrne, Bernard, blacksmith.

C

CADDELL, Edward, attorney and seneschal.
Campbell, Samuel, dealer.
Carr, Nicholas, tanner.
Cary, William, collector of taxes.
Christian, C. R. attorney.
Christian, Mrs.
Clark, Mrs. Jane, *Drumgumon.*
Clegg, Joseph, constable.
Corran, Charles, blacksmith.
Craig, John, farmer.
Creek, Jane, earthenware dealer.
Crory, Edward, crane-master.
Crummie, James, dealer.

D

DALZELL, Samuel, grocer.
Dalzell, Stuart, hosier.
Davidson, Arthur, publican and grocer.

Davidson, James, grocer.
Donnell, William, haberdasher.
Downey, Felix, currier.
Doyle, Roger, dealer.
Doyle, Patrick, butcher.
Duncan, James, shoemaker.
Duncan, Samuel, shoemaker.
Dunlap, Mrs. Margaret.

E

ENGLISH, John, publican.

F

FEGAN, John, farmer.
Fegan, Edward, farmer, *Barnmeen.*
Fegan, Terence, farmer, *Barnmeen.*
Fisher, J. shoemaker.
Fletcher, Rev. William, *Ballybrick.*
Flight, Sergeant, earthenware dealer.

G

GELSTON, William, plasterer.
Gilmore, Patrick, carpenter.
Gorman, Hugh, pump-maker.
Gowday, Hugh, carpenter.

H

HAGAN, Patrick, wheelwright.
Hagan, William, tailor.
Halyday, James, cabinet-maker.
Hart, Robert, wheelwright.

Hart, John, tallow chandler.
Hart, Hugh, painter and glazier.
Hawthorn, George, blacksmith.
Henan, Patrick, pump-maker.
Heron, John, grocer.
Hislop, Alexander, pensioner.
Hillan, John, nailer.
Hudson, Robert, reedmaker.

K

KEAN, Daniel, innkeeper.
Kean, Andrew, farmer.
Kennedy, Thomas, grocer.
Keown, Hugh, weaver.

L

LAWSON, William, butcher.
Leatham, James, hatter.
Lennon, Owen, baker.
Lennon, Bridget, dealer.
Lindsey, Miss Ann.

M

MACMULLEN, Rev. D. W.
Mageery, James, surgeon.
Marshall, Patrick, seal-master.
Martin, David, grocer.
May, Joseph, blue-dier.
May, Martha, grocer.
Miles, John, nailer.
Moore, Neal, dealer.
Morgan, Matthew, publican.

Morgan, Michael, flaxdresser,
Morgan, Patrick, dealer.
Morrison, Samuel, grocer.
Morrison, John, farmer.
Morrison, Mary, milliner.
Morrow, Hugh, farmer and linen-draper, *Banfort.*
Morrow, Edward, mason.
Murphy, Samuel, gent.
Murphy, John, gent. *Lackington.*
Murphy, Joseph, postmaster and woollen-draper.
Murphy, Robert, road-maker.
Musson, James, hosier.

M^c

M'Aleavy, John, mason.
M'Anuff, Robert, tailor.
M'Auley, Mary, milliner.
M'Avoy, Dominick, tailor.
M'Avoy, Hugh, tailor.
M'Burney, Robert, stonecutter.
M'Burney, Alexander, stonecutter.
M'Burney, George, stonecutter.
M'Burney, Thomas, stonecutter.
M'Cardle, J. schoolmaster.
M'Clean, Patrick, publican.
M'Clenahan, Andrew, grocer.
M'Cormick, James, mason.
M'Cracken, William, reedmaker.
M'Cullough, Robert, currier.
M'Donald, Patrick.
M'Donald, John, hosier.
M'Giveran, John, grocer.

M'Gregor, Daniel, tobacco-spinner.
M'Ilroy, Patrick, publican.
M'Ilwain, John, clock and watchmaker.
M'Kee, Robert, deputy supervisor of excise.
M'Keown, Patrick, shoemaker.
M'Keown, Tully, currier.
M'Keown, Hugh, weaver.
M'Mahon, Robert, publican.
M'Neill, Samuel, dealer,
M'Neilly, David, haberdasher.

N

NEWELL, Mrs. *King-hill.*

O

O'HAGAN, Bernard, tailor.
O'Hear, Patrick, tallow chandler.

P

PARKER, John, cooper.
Paxton, Richard, Esq. *Balaghashone.*
Penny, James, publican.

Q

QUINN, William, farmer.

R

RAIN, Samuel, farmer.
Rainey, Isaac, grocer.
Rowan, James, surgeon.

S

Scott, Thomas, Esq.
Scott, W. G. Esq.
Shaw, John, baker.
Shepard, James, grocer.
Sloan, Richard, dealer.
Soults, John, publican.
Stevenson, John, haberdasher.
Stevenson, Samuel, flaxdresser. Stewart, Rev. John.
Stewart, William, butcher.
Stewart, John, butcher.
Stewart, Hans, dealer.
Swan, John.
Swan, Samuel, surgeon.
Swan, William, farmer, *Grollogh*.

T

Tate, Rev. Thomas.
Thompson, Matthew, dealer.
Todd, James, gent.

W

Watt, William, publican.
White, Rev. John, *Bann-hill*.
Wier, Joseph, publican.
Willock, Miss Penelope.
Willock, H. S. gent.
Woods, Walter, tobacconist.
Wright, Henry, publican.

Y

Young, Robert, shoemaker.

DIRECTORY

OF

THE CITY OF ARMAGH

AND THE

ADJOINING TOWNS,

FOR 1819.

Historical Account of the City of Armagh.

Armagh, a city of Ulster, the ecclesiastical metropolis of Ireland, and the capital of the county of Armagh, is situated on a hill, surrounded by a highly cultivated and picturesque country, and within less than a quarter of a mile of the river Callan, to whose banks it once extended. It is the seat of the consistorial court of his grace the archbishop of Armagh, who is the primate and metropolitan of all Ireland. The see of Armagh extends into five counties, viz.—Armagh, Derry, Meath, Tyrone, and Louth, being 75 miles from north to south, and from 12½ to 32 in breadth.

Armagh was, in the middle centuries, an extensive and populous city, and was celebrated as a place of learning, having had, at one period, according to the Irish historians, seven thousand students at its college. The city, with the cathedral, a large Gothic building, one hundred and ninety feet from east to west, and one hundred and twenty-five from north to south, was built in the year 445, by St. Patrick. It was afterwards destroyed by fire, and ravaged by the Danes, who took off or annihilated the archieves of this ancient place. It was also often plundered or laid waste, in the repeated wars between the natives and the Anglo-Normans; and, in 1642, it was set on fire by Sir Phelim O'Neil. From the time of the suppression of the abbeys, with which Armagh abounded, it had dwindled into a very insignificant and neglected town; and in this state it remained until Dr. Richardson, afterwards Baron Rokeby, was promoted to the primacy. By the princely munificence of this prelate, the cathedral was repaired, and the town altogether renovated. He built and endowed an observatory, with an excellent astronomical apparatus, a library, and a palace, with a neat chapel, on the glebe adjacent to the city. To his liberality Armagh is also indebted for a parish school lately built, and for a school, where children are educated gratuitously, according to the modern improved systems. The school is in a flourishing condition, and is endowed with 1530 acres of fine land, which, in 1804, produced a gross annual rent of £1144 10s. 5½d.

A very elegant county court-house, in which the business of the assizes, quarter sessions, &c. is transacted, has been lately built, at the foot of the gentle acclivity on which the observatory stands. In front of this building, there are very pleasant public walks, surrounded by trees, planted in an eliptic form: these walks seem to be half encircled, on the eastern, northern and western points, by public buildings, while on the eastern side, the houses of the city appear ascending gradually one above the other, until the view is terminated by the cathedral.

A few years ago, a handsome church was erected, on a gentle acclivity, between the barracks and the free school.

On the western side of the city there is a charter-house or eleemosynary poor school, of considerable magnitude, founded in 1758. In addition to the churches already mentioned, the places of worship are, a large Presbyterian meeting-house, a meeting-house for Seceders, a tabernacle for the Evangelical congregation, a large Roman Catholic chapel, and two Methodist preaching-houses. The city, before the union, sent two members to parliament; it now sends only one.

In Armagh, an association for the suppression of mendicity was lately formed. It is supported by voluntary subscriptions. His Grace the Lord Primate contributes £50 per annum, and about £780 are subscribed by the inhabitants, by whom a committee has been appointed to manage the distribution of the money.—A society for the relief of sick poor meet once a week in the market-house, and appoint a number of persons out of their body to visit and relieve the indigent.—A short time since, a Savings Bank was established, under the most respectable gentlemen in the neighbourhood.

The county infirmary is a handsome edifice, situated at the junction of Abbey-street and Callan-street. The number of intern patients who receive surgical aid in this institution may be averaged at one hundred and sixty, and the extern patients who are supplied with medicine, at three thousand.

A public bakery has been lately established in English-street, which promises to be of considerable utility in regulating the assize of bread. The public news-room is situated in the same street.—From a basin convenient to the city, the inhabitants are supplied with water, which is conveyed by pipes into their dwelling houses, at the rate of £1 per annum.

Armagh has a very large market every Tuesday. The principal commodity sold in it is linen cloth in the brown state. The average weekly sales of this article amount to 7000 pieces, which, valued at £1 9s, per piece, would amount to £10,150. There is also a market every Saturday for grain and all kinds of provisions.

By a census taken a few years ago, the number of inhabitants are 7010, of which 2001 are of the established church; dissenters of different sects, 1501, chiefly Presbyterians, and 3413 Roman Catholics. Number of Houses, 1300. Distant from Dublin 62 miles, from Belfast 30, and from Newry 14½. Longitude, according to the most accurate observations, 6° 37′ 57″ west. Latitude, 54° 20′ 55″ north.

Directory of Armagh, for 1819.

A

Abbott, Richard, nailer, Barrack street.

Adams, John, haberdasher, English street.

Allen, John, attorney's clerk, English street.

Allot, Rev. Richard, librarian, Abbey street.

Anderson, Catherine, jeweller, Scotch street.

Anderson, John, carpenter, Market street.

Andrews, William, publican, *Linen Draper,* Scotch street.

Appleby, Thomas, licensed conveyancer, Abbey st.

Arbuthnot, Mrs. Vicars' hill.

Armstrong, James, solicitor, Abbey street.

Armstrong, William, land-surveyor, English street.

Armstrong, Henry, officer of excise, Abbey st.

Ashe, John, scrivener, Courthouse.

Atkinson, Edward, M. D. English street.

B

Baggot, Michael, clothes-dealer, Castle street.

Baker, Charles, thread lace manufacturer, English street.

Ball, Rev. William, rector of Dungannon, curate of Armagh, and surrogate of the diocess, English street.

Ballentine, Alexander, wheelwright, Callan street.

Bambrick, Wm. saddler and harness-maker, Scotch street.

Barns, William, tanner, Scotch street.

Barns, John, tanner, Scotch street.

Barr, Frances, seminary for young ladies, Thomas Street.

Barret, Edward, bootmaker, Thomas street.

Baxter, James, linen merchant, Scotch street.

Baxter, Moses, tinman, Irish street.

Baxter, Robert, carpenter, Abbey street.

Beatty, David, land steward to his Grace the Lord Primate, English street.

Beatty, James, baker, Scotch street.

Beggs, William, gent. College street.

Bell, William, Barrack street.

Bell, Matthew, flour merchant, English street.

Bell, James T. solicitor, Scotch street.

Bell, John, carman's inn, Scotch street.

Bell, John, landscape painter, Thomas street.

Bennet, Henry, tanner, English street.

Bennet, James, grocer and spirit-dealer, Market st.

Bently, Mr. *Palace.*

Blair, Robert, whitesmith, Irish street.

Blair, Francis, wheelwright, Thomas Street.

Blair, William, carpenter, Abbey street.

Blakely, David, gent. Abbey street.

Bolton, Abigail, post-mistress, Scotch street.

Boyd, Miss Mary, Abbey Street.

Boyd, Samuel, reedmaker, Barrack street.

Boyd, Mrs. Ann, English street.

Boyd, William, grocer, Thomas street.

Boyd, Matthew, thread manufacturer and coal and iron merchant, Thomas street.

Boyd, Joseph, carpenter, charter-school lane.

Boyle, John, shoemaker, Thomas street.

Bradley, James, grocer, Thomas Street.

Brady, William, boot and shoemaker, College st.

Brawley, James, schoolmaster, Irish Street.

Brennan, William, skinner, English street.

Bright, Samuel, confectioner, English street.

Bright, Ann, confectioner, Thomas street.

Brocas, William, preceptor of music, English st.

Brothers, Thomas, Market street.

Brown, William, merchant; house, English street.

Brown, John, publican, *Duke of Wellington,* Scotch street.

Brown, John, town-serjeant, Callan street.

Brown, John, saddler and harness-maker, Thomas street.

Byers, John, Belfast coachman, Scotch street.

Byrne, Mrs. Catherine, Scotch street.

Byrne, Henry, publican, Thomas street.

Byrne, George, gardner, Dobbin street.

C

CALLAGHAN, Owen, leather seller, Market street.

Callaghan, Terence, brogue-maker, Irish street.

Caldwell, Johntson, accountant, English street.

Caldwell, C. & T. grocers, English street.

Caldwell, Elizabeth, publican, English street.

Calter, Eliza, publican, Irish street.

Campbell, Thomas, Abbey street.

Campbell, James, M. D. Vicars' hill.

Campbell, Rev. Henry, P. P. and Vicar General of the
    District, Abbey street.

Campbell, Florence, cooper, Jenny's row.

Campbell, Mrs. Jane, Vicars' hill.

Campbell, William, grocer and tobacconist, Scotch street.

Campbell, Edward, carpenter, English street.

Carlow, Margaret, straw bonnet manufacturer, Barrack
    street.

Carlow, Margaret, publican, Market street.

Carpendale, Mrs. Jane, English street.

Carroll, Wm. grocer and, spirit merchant, English street.

Carroll, Richard, gardener, Abbey street.

Cassiday, William, hatter, Charter-school lane.

Cavanagh, Charles, grocer, Irish street.

Christian, Christopher, hosier and haberdasher, Thomas street.

Christy, Peter, boot and shoemaker, Scotch street.

Clark, Archibald, tailor, Dobbin street.

Clegg, Francis, blacksmith, Barrack street.

Cleland, Rev. John, rector of Drumbanagher, Abbey street.

Clore, James, haberdasher, English street.

Close, Bernard, haberdasher, English street.

Cochran, Robert, grocer, soap-boiler and tallow chandler, English street.

Cochran, Mrs. Sarah, English street.

Cochran, Robert, jun. grocer and spirit merchant, English street.

Cochran, John, professor of sacred music, Barrack street.

Colclough, Maria, baker and dressmaker, Barrack street.

Coleman, Rev. Peter, R. C. P. Castle street.

Coleman, John, carpenter, Callan street.

Collins, James, clothes-dealer, church lane.

Colven, John, baker, Scotch street.

Colven, John. jun. surgeon, Scotch street.

Colven, Philip, English street.

Conlin, Henry, tailor, English street.

Connor, Margaret, publican, *Black Bull*, Barrack street.

Connolly, Edward, yarn merchant, Thomas street.

Connolly, Patrick, gardener, Charter-school lane.

Convill, Anthony, farmer, Church lane.

Conway, Robert, carpenter, English street.

Corr, Felix, huxter, Castle street.

Corran, John, shoemaker, Chapel lane.

Corrigan, Meredith, haberdasher, Market street.

Corrigan, James, haberdasher, Market street.

Corry, George, woollendraper and spirit-dealer, Market street.

Corry, Mrs. Barbara, English street.

Corry, James, pedler, English street.

Corven, Edward, sen. English street.

Corven, Patrick, grocer, English street.

Cosgrave, Mark, cooper, English street.

Cosgrave, James, gardener, Castle street.

Coyle, Paul, tailor, Castle street.

Craig, Samuel, wholesale and retail ironmonger and hardware merchant, Scotch street.

Cranmer, Mary, clothes-dealer, Castle street.

Crawley, — saddler, Thomas street.

Creely, James, huxter, Castle street.

Crummy, Edward, carpenter, Castle street.

Crummy, Neal, grocer and leather-seller, Castle st.

Cullen, Bernard, blacksmith, Irish street.

Cullen, John, clock and watchmaker, Thomas St.

Cully, John, pawnbroker and commission agent, Thomas street.

Cuming, James, soap-boiler and tallow chandler, Barrack street.

Cumming, Mrs. Elizabeth, Abbey street.

D

Dalzell, Nathaniel, Barrack street.

Dalzell, Richardson, leather-seller, Market street.

Darlington, Richard, steward to Lord Lifford, *Tulladegny*.

Davis, Walter, baker, Barrack street.

Davis, John, meal-dealer, Dobbin street.

Dawson, Henry, gardener, Callan street.

Delany, Peter, millwright, Castle street.

Devlin, Patrick, grocer and publican, English st.

Devlin, Owen, publican, English street.

Devlin, Arthur, mason, English street.

Devall, Joseph, hair-dresser, English street.

Dickson, Sir Jeremiah, Seven houses, English st.

Dickson, Elizabeth, publican, *Cross Keys,* Scotch st.

Dobbin, Leonard, Esq. Scotch street.

Dobbin, Leonard, jun. solicitor, Seven houses, English street.

Donaghy, Peter, shoemaker, Primrose lane.

Donnelly, Daniel, clock and watchmaker, English street.

Donnelly, Thomas, land surveyor, English street.

Donnelly, James, publican, English street.

Donnelly, Thomas, tailor, Barrack street.

Donnelly, Peter, huxter, English street.

Donnelly, Hugh, tailor, Thomas street.

Donnelly, Patrick, miller, Chapel lane.

Donnelly, Peter, meal-dealer, Charter-school lane.

Donnelly, Terence, flaxdresser, Abbey lane.

Doon, Arthur, shoemaker, Irish street.

Dougherty, John, whitesmith, Abbey lane.

Dowd, John, nailer, Abbey street.

Dowd, James, shoemaker, English street.

Dowd, Lawrence, sawyer, Abbey street.

Downey, Neal, fruit-seller, English street.

Drum, Hugh C. fancy chair-maker, Thomas st.

Duffy, Nicholas, coachman, Market street.

Duffy, James, baker, Castle street.

Duffy, Edward, slater, Chapel lane.

Duffy, Thomas, butcher, Chapel lane.

Dugan, Michael, shoemaker, Abbey lane.

Dugan, Anthony, shoemaker, Chapel lane.

Duncan, John, clock and watchmaker, English street.

Dunleavy, James, butcher, Chapel lane.
Dunleavy, Thomas, tailor, Primrose lane.
Dunn, James, English street.
Dunn, William, nailer, English street.
Durham, James, news-room, English street.

E

EAGER, Thomas, shoemaker, Charter-school lane.
Eccles, Rev. Samuel, Presbyterian minister, Market street.
Edgar, Rev. S. C. Seceding minister, Abbey st.
Elliott, Thomas, plasterer, Primrose lane.
Enoah, Christopher, cabinet-maker and upholsterer,
    Thomas street.
Eves, John Wilcocks, cabinet-maker, English st.
Ewing, John, carpenter, Abbey street.
Ewing, Samuel, blacksmith, Abbey street.
Ewing, William, blacksmith, Abbey street.

F

FANNEN, Edward, carpenter, Barrack street.
Feely, James, butcher, English street.
Feenan, John, saddler and harness-maker.
Fegan, Arthur, farmer, Abbey lane.
Ferguson, James, publican, English street.
Ferguson, Mrs. Rachael, Vicars' hill.
Ferrian, John, carpenter, English street.
Fitzsimmons, James, shoemaker, Irish street.
Fitzsimmons, Christopher, mason, Irish street.
Flanagan, Daniel, yarn merchant, Castle street.
Flanngan, Thomas, butcher, Castle street.
Foster, Charles, serjeant. English street.
Foster, J. M. book-keeper, English street.

G

Gallagher, John, pawnbroker, Market street.

Gallagher, John, stocking merchant, Charter-school lane.

Garbett, John, professor of music, Vicars' hill.

Gardner, Samuel and William, woollendrapers and agents to the British and Irish United Fire and Westminster Insurance Company, Market st.

Gardner, William, straw hat manufacturer, Market street.

Garland, Robert, slater, Primrose lane.

Garland, George, slater, Irish street.

Garvey, John, baker, Castle street.

Garvey, Hugh, publican, English street.

Garvey, Robert, baker, English street.

Geary, John, publican, Market street.

Gibson, John, tobacco-spinner, Primrose lane.

Gibson, Thomas, huxter, Barrack street.

Girvin, Mrs. Sarah, Dobbin street.

Gordon, James, shoemaker, Barrack street.

Gough, William, Castle street.

Graham, Patrick, mealmonger, Abbey street.

Graham, John, grocer, English street.

Graham, James, Scotch street.

Grant, Peter, huxter, Thomas street.

Gray, John, hat manufacturer, Thomas street.

Gribbin, James, publican, Irish street.

Griffith, Judith, publican, *King's Arms,* English st.

Grimley, Terence, baker, Castle street.

Guerin, Henry, professor of the French language, Abbey street.

H

Hacket, Cornelius, sawyer, Abbey street.

Haddock, John, attorney, Irish street.

Haddock, James, grocer, Thomas street.

Hagan, Daniel, tailor, Castle street.

Hagan, John, flaxdresser, Irish street.

Hall, George, porter to his Grace the Lord Primate.

Hall, William, huxter, Irish street.

Halligan, William, fruiterer, Abbey street.

Halligan, James, lodging-house, Church street.

Hamilton, David, vicar choral of St. Patrick's, Vicars' hill.

Hamilton, George, eating-house, Scotch street.

Hamilton, Robert, hair-dresser and perfumer, Thomas street.

Hammond, Richard, lodging-house, Castle street.

Hanley, John, clothes-dealer, Market street.

Hanlon, Ardle, carpenter, Thomas street.

Hancock, Jane, grocer, English street.

Harrington, William and Robert, grocers, and wine and spirit merchants, Market street.

Hart, James, publican, Scotch street.

Hart, John, whitesmith, Irish street.

Harvey, Mrs. Ann, Thomas street.

Harvey, Thomas, mealmonger, Charter-school lane.

Healy, Thomas, whip-maker, English street.

Healy, Thomas, corn merchant, Callan street.

Healy, Thomas, mealmonger, Irish street.

Hearse, Thomas, excise officer, English street.

Heir, Hugh, lodging-house, Chapel lane.

Henan, John, huxter, Callan street.

Henderson, Richard, whitesmith, Market street.

Henry, Robert, surgeon, Thomas street.

Henry, Thomas, publican, *Coach & Horses,* Scotch street.

Henry, John, cabinet-maker & upholsterer, Scotch street.

Henry, William, painter and glazier, Market street.

Henry, William, publican, *Struggler,* Market st.

Henry, John, sealmaster, Thomas street.

Heyland, John, shoemaker, Chapel lane.

Hillock, Charles, carpenter and master builder, Barrack street.

Hillan, Peter, dealer, English street.

Hogg, Rev. Robert, astronomer, Scotch street.

Hollywood, Patrick, farmer, English street.

Horncastle, T. W. organist of the cathedral, Vicars' hill.

Houston, Rev. Francis, English street.

Houston, Thomas, blue-dier, Charter-school lane.

Howden, Rev. William, Independent minister, Dobbin street.

Hughes, Felix, cattle-dealer, Irish street.

Hughes, Arthur, bootmaker, Scotch street.

Hughes, George, bootmaker, English street.

Hughes, Henry, baker and flour-dealer, English st.

Hughes, Patrick, publican, Castle street.

Hughes, Andrew, dealer, Castle street.

Hughes, Patrick, mealmonger, Abbey street.

I

ILES, James, Esq. sovereign, Seven houses.

Ingram, Sampson, Dobbin street.

Irwin, William, haberdasher, Scotch street.

Irwin, James, skinner, English street.

Irwin, Mrs. E. English street.

Irwin, Patten, carpenter, Barrack street.

J

JAKSON,[*sic*] Robert and Son, flour merchants, Market street.

Jackson, John, coal merchant, Abbey street.

Johnston, Mrs. Primrose lane.

Johnston, John, bell-hanger, Primrose lane.

Johnston, Robert, boot and shoemaker, Thomas st.

Johnston, James, hosier, Barrack street.

Jones, John, auctioneer, Barrack street.

Jones, William, skinner, Thomas st.

K

KANE, John, woollendraper and wholesale printed calico warehouse, Market street.

Karney, John, Barrack street.

Kays, Charles, sergeant at mace, Palace row.

Kays, Charles, jun. collector of customs, Palace row.

Kearney, Lieut. Col. Abbey street.

Kearney, James, Esq. barrack-master.

Kearney, Patrick, carrier, English street.

Kearney, James, tailor, Church street.

Kearns, Thomas, leather-seller, Thomas street.

Keaten, Bernard, baker, Irish street.

Kelly, Arthur I. Esq. Rokeby green, College St.

Kelly, Bernard, grocer, Barrack street.

Kelly, Edward, baker, English street.

Kelly, James, flaxdresser, English street.

Kelly, Bernard, woollendraper, Market street.

Kelly, John, baker, Thomas street.

Kelly, John, gardener, Irish street.

Kelly, Maurice, hatter, Chapel lane.

Kelly, Mrs. Mary Ann, Seven houses.

Kerr, John, commission agent, Abbey street.

Kidd, William Lodge, M. D. Vicars' hill.

Kidd, T. and O. flour merchants, English street.

Kidd, Hugh, flour merchants, English street.

Kirk, William, linen merchant, Scotch street.

Kitson, John, huxter and brick-maker, Barrack St.

L

LAMB, Charles, gardener to his Grace the Lord Primate.

Lane, Matilda, haberdasher, English street.

Lang, Mary, calico manufacturer and haberdasher, Thomas street.

Langley, Mrs. Jane, English street.

Lappan, Miss Catherine, Scotch street.

Lappan, Jane, publican, Barrack street.

Lappan, William, Abbey lane.

Lappan, John, ropemaker.

Lee, John, gent. Charter-school lane.

Lee, Elizabeth, hotel and tavern, *Roe Buck*, Scotch street.

Lee, Malcom, publican, English street.

Lee, John, grocer and spirit-dealer, Scotch street.

Lee, Oliver, ironmonger, Thomas street.

Leslie, William, gun-maker, Scotch street.

Lester, Robert, grocer, Thomas street.

Lindley, Thomas, bookseller, stationer and Jeweller, Scotch street.

Lindsay, Richard, baker, Scotch street.

Lindsay, Margaret, clothes-dealer, Market street.

Linton, Walsh, reed-maker, Thomas street.

Livingston, Robert, Esq. English street.

Logan, Patrick, tanner, Chapel lane.

Long, John, huxter, Market street.

Loughran, Cornelius, schoolmaster, Thomas Street.

Lowe, Henry, Innkeeper, grocer, &c. *Cotton Tree, Mountnorris.*

Lowry, Patrick, nailer, Barrack street.

Lucas, Andrew, boot and shoemaker, Thomas street.
Lucas, James, combmaker, Thomas street.
Lyle, Andrew, sen. gent. English street.
Lyle, Andrew, jun. brewer, English street.

M

MAGEE, Michael, coroner, commissioner for taking
affidavits for his Majesty's Four Courts, and for taking
special bail for the courts of King's Bench and Common
Pleas, and deputy clerk of the peace, Rokeby green.
Magee, John, carpenter, Abbey lane.
Magleenan, Jane, baker, Scotch street.
Maguire, Thomas, assistant barrackmaster, Barrack.
Maguire, Thomas, shoemaker, English street.
Mahan, Edward, mason, Irish street.
Mallon, James, tailor, Thomas street.
Maloy, Matthew, wheelwright, Castle street.
Marsh, William, cook to his Grace the Lord Primate.
Martin, Patrick, mason, Abbey street.
Martin, James, broguemaker, Irish street.
Mathews, Mrs. Elizabeth, Barrack street.
Maul, Jane, haberdasher and straw bonnet-maker, English
street.
Maxwell, James, ironmonger, Market street.
Maziere, Andrew, apothecary, Market street.
Malone, Richard, publican, English street.
Miller, Rev. George, D. D. president of the college.
Miller, John, grocer, Scotch street.
Minnes, John, wholesale and retail grocer, &c. &c. Scotch
street.
Mosby, Thomas, butcher, English street.
Monks, James, butcher, English street.

Montgomery, William, farmer, Dobbin street.

Mooney, Matthew, broguemaker, Irish street.

Moorhead, Miss Sarah, school-mistress, Callan st.

Moren, James, confectioner, Scotch street.

Morrison, Thomas, tailor, English street.

Moss, Robert, butcher to his Grace the Lord Primate.

Mosson, William, boot and shoemaker, Thomas st.

Mullen, Mary Ann, huxter, Barrack street.

Murphy, Terence, dealer, English street.

Murphy, Edward, gardener, English street.

Murphy, Patrick, carpenter, Barrack street.

Murphy, Anthony, sawyer, Abbey lane.

Murray, John, schoolmaster, English street.

Murray, William, tailor, Palace row.

Murray, Thomas, shoemaker, Abbey street.

Murray, Richard, gent. Abbey street.

Murtaugh, John, baker, Irish street.

Mᶜ

M'Bride, Michael, publican, English street.

M'Cabe, John, flaxdresser, Abbey street.

M'Caffry, James, shoemaker, Church lane.

M'Cahey, Peter, carman's inn, Barrack street.

M'Call, Matthew, lodging-house, Irish street.

M'Cann, Robert, meal and flour-dealer, Scotch st.

M'Cann, John, eating-house, Scotch street.

M'Cann, Owen, huxter, Castle street.

M'Cann, John, corn and meal-dealer, Thomas st.

M'Cann, Neal, dealer, Chapel lane.

M'Cann, Thomas, painter and glazier, Charter-school lane.

M'Cann, Thomas, mealmonger. Primrose lane.

M'Cann, Thomas, huxter, Thomas street.

M'Caragher, John, dealer, Market street.

M'Cardle, Patrick, blacksmith, English street.

M'Cardle, John, carrier, Irish street.

M'Carter, Samuel, shoemaker, Church lane.

M'Cluny, Alexander, chandler, Thomas street.

M'Cluny, Samuel, chandler, Irish street.

M'Clure, Joseph, grocer and spirit-dealer, Scotch street.

M'Coal, Lawrence, shoemaker, English street.

M'Cone, Patrick, publican, Irish street.

M'Connell, Matthew, clerk, Barrack street.

M'Connell, Archibald, cartmaker and manufacturer of
farming utensils, Rokeby green.

M'Cormick, Ann, seminary for young ladies, College street.

M'Cormick, Miss E. College street.

M'Cormick, Dominick, hair-dresser, Scotch street.

M'Court, Thomas, carpenter, English street.

M'Court, Patrick, carpenter, Market street.

M'Court, James, tailor, Jenny's row.

M'Cready, Andrew, nailer, Church lane.

M'Creesh, John, mason, Callan street.

M'Crum, Mrs. Margaret, Scotch street.

M'Crum. William, manufacturer of linen yarn, by
machinery, *Millford*.

M'Crum, Nathaniel, corn-miller and farmer, *Lismalow*.

M'Cullough, Mrs. Elizabeth, Dobbin street.

M'Cully, Hugh, gent. College street.

M'Cully, Bernard, clothes-dealer, Castle street.

M'Cune, James, College street.

M'Cutchen, Charles, cartmaker, Palace row.

M'Donnell, Peter, mealmonger, Irish street.

M'Donnell, Samuel, tailor, Abbey street.

M'Donnell, Alexander, drover, Scotch street.

M'Donnell, Edward, butcher, Thomas street.

M'Dowell, John, carpenter, Rokeby green.

M'Endow, Robert, schoolmaster, Abbey street.

M'Farlin, Charles, grocer, Thomas street.

M'Garrity, Philip, shoemaker, Market street.

M'Garrity, John, publican, *Friendly Brothers,* Scotch street.

M'Geough, Patrick, baker, Thomas street.

M'Gorelake, Mary, billiard-room, Scotch street.

M'Gorelake, Mary, ball-court, Callan street.

M'Gowan, Samuel, tailor, Thomas street.

M'Gowan, Patrick, brogue-maker, Chapel lane.

M'Gowan, Dennis, brogue-maker, Chapel lane.

M'Grath, James, carpenter, Irish street.

M'Guigan, Francis, gardener, Callan street.

M'Gurk, Patrick, clothes-dealer, Castle street.

M'Ilroy, Alexander, carpenter, Market street.

M'Ilroy, James, mason, English street.

M'Ilroy, John, mason, English street.

M'Kean, Robert, grocer and spirit merchant, Market street.

M'Kean, Henry, woollendraper and haberdasher, Market street.

M'Kean, Jane, innkeeper, Scotch street.

M'Kearnan, Felix, mason, Charter-school lane.

M'Kee, Dennis, publican, *Red Lion,* Scotch st.

M'Kee, Thomas, huxter, Scotch street.

M'Kee, Francis, leather-seller, Castle street.

M'Kee, Francis, mealmonger, Castle street.

M'Kelvy, William, wheelwright and turner.

M'Kelvy, John, servant, Abbey street.

M'Kenna, John, hostler, Abbey street.

M'Kenna, Patrick, breeches-maker, Jenny's row.

M'Kenny, Michael, huxter, Barrack street.

M'Kew, Robert, register to the metropolitan, *Rose brook.*

M'Key, John, nailer, Irish street.

M'Killop, George, linen merchant, Scotch street.

M'Kinstry, Lee, solicitor, Scotch street.

M'Kinstry and Kidd, flour merchants, English st.

M'Kinstry, Robert, clerk of the peace, English st.

M'Laughlin, Henry, shoemaker, Primrose lane.

M'Laughlin, Bernard, mason, Irish street.

M'Laughlin, Daniel, mason, English street.

M'Laughlin, James, mason, Abbey street.

M'Mahon, Owen, clothes-dealer, Castle street.

M'Mahon, Philip, mason, Abbey street.

M'Manus, Patrick, carpenter, Irish street.

M'Master, Charles, proctor, Castle street.

M'Murray, Hugh, carpenter, Abbey lane.

M'Nair, William, publican, *Duke of York,* Market street.

M'Phie, John, huxter, Barrack street.

M'Reidy, Patrick, mealmonger, Abbey street.

M'Shadden, John, surgeon, Market street.

M'Shane, Peter, butcher, Primrose lane.

M'Sorley, Randall, flaxdresser, Charter-school lane.

M'Williams, Wm. grocer and tobacconist, Scotch street.

M'Williams, William, gent. English street.

M'William, John, publican, *Nelson and Abercrombie,* English
street.

N

Neilus, Charles, blacksmith, Irish street.

Nelson, William, shoemaker, Irish street.

Nelson, Samuel, shoemaker, Irish street.

Newbanks, Henry, blacksmith, Abbey lane.

Newton, Michael, butler.

Niblock, Richard, saddler and harness-maker, Thomas
street.

Noble, John, high constable, Church lane.
Norris, Richard, shoemaker, Primrose lane.
Nugent, James, stone and marble yard, Abbey st.

O

O'DONNELL, Charles, cooper, Callan street.
O'Hagan, Francis, painter and glazier to his Grace the Lord
　　Primate, Barrack street.
O'Hare, Bernard, currier, Chapel lane.
O'Kane, Thomas, Callan street.
Oliver, William, farmer, Thomas street.
Olpherts, Mrs. Barbara, Abbey street.
O'Neill, Hugh, tanner, Thomas street.
O'Neill, Owen, butcher, Irish street.
O'Neill, Charles, mealmonger, Abbey street.
O'Neill, Hugh, butcher, Callan street.
Orr, Daniel, manufacturing jeweller, Scotch street.

P

PALMER, Arthur, Esq. R. N. English street.
Palmer, John, leather-seller, Thomas, street.
Palmer, Rachael, haberdasher and milliner, Scotch street.
Pasmore, George, huxter, Scotch street.
Peebles, Robert, currier, English street.
Penton, William, nursery and seedsman, Thomas street.
Plunket, William, publican, English street.
Pollock, Joseph, Esq. English street.
Pooler, William, printer, bookseller and stationer, Scotch
　　street.
Powell, Major, English street.
Prentice, Alexander, merchant and tobacconist, Scotch
　　street.

Prentice, George, spirit, oil, paint and colour merchant, Scotch street.

Prentice, Mrs. Rose, Scotch street.

Prunty, Agnes, clothes-dealer, Castle street.

Q

QUIGLY, Hugh, town-sergeant, Callan street.

Quin, Thomas & Hugh, grocers and spirit-dealers, English street.

Quin, John, carpenter, English street.

Quin, Dennis, huxter, Thomas street.

R

REA, James, gardener at Mr. Penton's nursery, Monaghan road.

Reid, James, lodging house, Market street.

Reilly, Connor, currier, Church lane.

Reilly, James, tin-plate worker, Thomas street.

Reilly, John, boot and shoemaker, Thomas street.

Rice, John, flaxdresser, Irish street.

Rice, Henry, flaxdresser, Irish street.

Rickard, John, baker, Abbey street.

Richardson, John, chandler, Thomas street.

Robinson, Miss Elizabeth, Abbey street.

Robinson, William, hosier, Thomas street.

Rocks, Patrick, huxter, Thomas street.

Rocks, Michael, butcher, Irish street.

Rogers, James, nailer.

Ross, John, shoemaker, Castle street.

Rowan, Samuel, linen merchant, Scotch street.

Rowan, Andrew, shoemaker, Chapel lane.

Rutherford, John, painter and glazier, Barrack st.

Ryan, Rev. Alexander, Abbey street.

Ryan, William, M. D. Abbey street.

Ryan, John, brogue-maker, Irish street.

S

SAVAGE, George, Irish street.

Savage, Henry, publican, Thomas street.

Savage, James, mason, Abbey lane.

Scarlett, David, master of the Primate's free school, Rokeby green.

Scarlett, Letitia, mistress of the Primate's free school, Rokeby green.

Scott, William, tin-plate worker, English street.

Scott, Robert, tailor, English street.

Scott, William, tailor, Callan street.

Scott, Robert, tin-plate worker, Thomas street.

Seymour, Thomas, whitesmith, Abbey lane.

Seymour, James, sawyer, Abbey lane.

Shaw, Major, Thomas street.

Sherry, Lawrence, boot and shoemaker, Thomas street.

Sherry, William, shoemaker, Abbey lane.

Short, Bernard, huxter, Thomas street.

Simpson, John, grocer and spirit-dealer, Market street.

Simpson, Thomas, flour merchant, Thomas street.

Slevin, Francis, saddler & harness-maker, English street.

Sling, John, hair-dresser, Thomas street.

Sling, Henry, hair-dresser, Thomas street.

Sloan, James, surgeon and apothecary, English st.

Sloan, John, oil and colour merchant, English st.

Sloan, Mary, deal yard, &c. English street.

Sloan, John, hosier, Abbey lane.

Smith, William, schoolmaster, Irish street.

Smith, James, gardener and seeds-man, English st.

Smith, William, shoemaker, Market street.

Spellman, Dennis, brogue-maker, Irish street.

Spence, William, book agent, Market street.

Sproull, Wilson, woollen-draper and haberdasher, Market
street.

Stanley, John, merchant, Seven houses; stores, College street.

Stanley, James, wholesale and retail grocer, wine and spirit
merchant, Scotch street.

Starr, Archibald, farmer, English street.

Starr, James, publican, Market street.

Steel, Robert, cabinet-maker, English street.

Stephen, James, tanner, English street.

Stephens, Thomas, smith and farrier, Thomas st.

Stevenson, Robert, printer, bookseller and stationer, Scotch
street.

Strawbridge, John, gent. Irish street.

Stratten, Isabella, chop-house, Scotch street.

Stuart, William, farmer, Thomas street.

Summerville, John, publican, *Nelson's Arms,* Scotch street.

T

TAYLOR, Hugh, Barrack street.

Taylor, John, millwright, *Glen Anne.*

Thompson, James, gent. Barrack street.

Thompson, Samuel, carpenter, English street.

Thompson, Robert, plumber, Abbey street.

Thornton, R. J. Esq. College street.

Treanor, Ann, publican, Thomas street.

Treanor, Hugh, clothes-dealer, Market street.

Treanor, Hugh, grocer and spirit-dealer, English street.

Turner, John, gaoler, Barrack street.

Tyrrell, Gerald, copper and tin-plate worker, Thomas street.

V

VALLALEY, Arthur, butcher, Irish street.
Vogan, Joshua, surgeon and apothecary, Market st.

W

WAINRIGHT, Robert, nailer, Thomas street.
Walker, Thomas, mason, English street.
Walsh, Lewis, lodging-house, Market street.
Walsh, James, brogue-maker, Charter-school lane.
Warwick, Armour, tailor, Scotch street.
Waugh, John, gent. English street.
Webster, Hugh, reedmaker, Charter-school lane.
Webster, James, reedmaker, Barrack street.
Wendrum, Mrs. Anne, Dobbin street.
White, Hugh, gent. Abbey street.
Whittington, Charles, gent. English street.
Whittington, Richard, grocer, spirit merchant and tallow
    chandler, Irish street.
Wier, James, carpenter, Palace row.
Wild, Capt. Benjamin, Scotch street.
Williams, John, book-keeper, English street.
Williamson, John, china, glass and earthenware merchant,
    English street.
Williamson, Hugh, scrivener, Thomas street.
Wilson, Robert, Thomas street.
Wilson, John, glass, china and earthenware dealer, Thomas
    street.
Wilson, Mrs. Abigail, Barrack street.
Wilton, Thomas, blue-dier, Castle street.
Wilton, Nicholas, nailer, Abbey lane.

Wilton, George, nailer, Irish street.
Winder, John, Esq. Abbey street.
Winder, Joseph, whitesmith, Abbey lane.
Woods, Michael, mason, Chapel lane.
Wright, Samuel, blacksmith, Barrack street.
Wright, Thomas, blacksmith, English street.

Y

Young, John, printer, bookbinder and stationer, Market
  street.
Young, Sarah, pawnbroker, Church lane.

Directory of Markethill, for 1819.

B

Barker, Captain of the Armagh staff.
Barker, Arthur, tailor.
Bradford, Benjamin, Esq.
Brooks, Charles, shoemaker.
Burrows, John, saddler.

C

Carroll, Matthew, mason.
Clark, Rev. James.
Connor, Thomas, shoemaker.
Connor, Thomas, butcher.
Corrigan, Henry, huxter.
Coulter, Alexander, hosier.
Craig, Alexander, tailor.
Cumings, Thomas, shoemaker.

D

Davis, Thomas, dealer in flax.

F

Feran, Sylvester, confectioner.

G

Gillis, Joseph, woollendraper.
Glassy, Brent, butcher.
Gordon, Samuel, woollendraper.
Gosford, the Right Hon. Earl of, *Gosford Castle.*
Graham, Thomas, shoemaker.
Gray, John, innkeeper, *King's Arms.*
Gray, Francis, farmer.
Gray, Alexander, carpenter.
Greer, James, blue-dier.

H

Hanlon, William, flaxdresser.

I

Irwin, John, publican.

J

Jephson, Rev. Mr. *Mullabrack.*

K

Kay, Arthur, Esq.

L

Lennon, Daniel, butcher.

M

Martin, William, Esq. *Mullabrack.*
Martin, William, huxter.
Mason, Daniel, leather-seller.

Mitcher, John, agent to the Earl of Gosford, *Gosford castle.*
Monypeny, David, gent.
Monypeny, Charles, woollendraper.
Monypeny, J. post-mistress, grocer and spirit-dealer.

Mᶜ

M'CALL, John, grocer and tallow chandler.
M'Creary, John, publican.
M'Creary, Thomas, grocer.
M'Kee, Bernard, linendraper.
M'Kenna, J. blacksmith.
M'Mahon, Thomas, reedmaker.
M'Nally, Mrs.
M'Parlin, Michael, publican, *Sun.*
M'Roberts, James, weaver.

N

NEAL, Henry, wheelwright.

O

O'HEAR, John, shoemaker.
O'Neill, Paul, wheelwright.
Ougheltree, Robert, hardwareman.
Ougheltree, David, publican.

P

PIDGEON, Edward, cooper.
Pollard, Matthew, grocer.

R

RANKIN, Joseph, shoemaker.
Robinson, George, huxter.

S

Scott, William, publican.
Sheals, Bernard, flaxdresser.
Sinclair, Archibald, linendraper.
Sinclair, George, surgeon.
Stretton, Mrs. innkeeper, *Grapes*.
Stuart, Daniel, reedmaker.

T

Thompson, James, huxter.
Thompson, James, gunsmith.

W

Walker, Arthur, painter and glazier.
Wann, John, steward to Lord Gosford.
Wilson, Joseph, surgeon and apothecary.
Woodhouse, Ralph, grocer.

HISTORICAL ACCOUNT OF THE
TOWN OF PORTADOWN.

PORTADOWN, in the barony of O'Neiland-West, in the county of Armagh, is a small town, containing about one hundred houses and nine hundred inhabitants. It is pleasantly seated on the western bank of the river Bann, over which there is an excellent bridge of thirteen arches. In the reign of Charles I. it consisted only of four houses, and was at that time called Portnedown. It lies about nine miles from Armagh, fifteen from Newry, twenty-two from Belfast, and six from Lough Neagh. In the year 1631, the estate on which the town stands was granted by Charles I. to John and Prudence Obins, in which family it still remains.

About twenty years ago, a number of handsome brick houses and extensive stores, were added to the town, which has since been much enlarged by a very neat row of houses, two stories high, built by Curran Woodhouse, Esq. At the west end of the town, there is a neat Methodist chapel which is the only house of public worship in Portadown.—The parish church and the Roman Catholic chapel of Drumcree are situated at a distance of one mile from the town.

In the year 1780, a wheat, and indeed, a general grain market, was established by the late Major Obins and George Wood-house, Esq. which has rapidly encreased, and is now equal to any in the north of Ireland. It is computed that about five thousand tons of wheat are annually purchased in this market, and re-sold to the several millers, in the county of Antrim, &c. Besides this, a considerable quantity of grain is shipped for England and Scotland, by Curran Woodhouse, Esq. Messrs. John Atkinson, Thomas Shillington, Wm. Overend, Roger Marley, &c. &c. There is also a good linen and yarn market in Portadown, every Saturday, and a monthly fair for the sale of cattle, on the third Saturday in each month. Annual fairs are likewise held on Easter Monday, Whit-Monday, and the first Monday in November. There is a distillery and two breweries in the town; but at present neither of them are in use.

Directory of Portadown, for 1819.

A

Armstrong, Christopher, haberdasher and spirit merchant.
Arnold, Elizabeth, huxter,
Atkins, Henry, innkeeper, *Obins's Arms*.
Atkinson, Woolsey, gent.
Atkinson John, merchant.
Anglow, George, weaver.

B

Black, William, shoemaker.
Black, Ann, huxter.
Bradford, Jane, haberdasher.
Bulla, Joshua, cabinet-maker.
Bunton, Thomas, carpenter.

C

Carnaghan, Elizabeth, huxter.
Carr, John, carpenter.
Carroll, Elinor, huxter.
Carter, James, butcher.
Carter, Edward, mason.
Christy, James, gunsmith.
Connor, Edward, shoemaker.
Costello, John, mason.
Cox, Peter, cooper.

Cull, John, hatter.
Curran, Mary, huxter.

D

Dawson, Thomas, publican.
Devlin, Dudley, publican.
Dickson, Miss Alice.
Dickson, Margaret, haberdasher.
Dodds, George, publican.
Dogherty, Robert, music-master.
Dougan, James, shoemaker.
Doyle, Mary, spinster.
Duck, Edward, publican.
Duffy, Hugh, labourer.

E

Evans, George, pensioner.
Ewing, James, carpenter.

F

Feenan, John, carrier.
Ferris, John, huxter.
Fisher, William, farmer.
Fowler, James, tinman.
Fowler, Claudius, labourer.

G

Gallagher, Patrick, linendraper.
Gibson, John, labourer.
Gilmore, Joseph, tallow chandler.
Green, Joseph, nailer.

H

HAGAN, Bernard, book-keeper.
Halligan, James, constable.
Hamilton, John, yarn dealer.
Hanlon, John, mason.
Hanna, James, publican.
Harrison, William, woollendraper.
Hart, James, publican.
Haughton, James, butcher.
Heburn, George, blacksmith.
Houston, John, sub-constable.
Houston, Robert, gardener.
Hudson, Hanna, flaxdresser.

I

IRWIN, William, accountant.
Irwin, Samuel, publican.

J

JOICE, William and John, grocers and Woollen-drapers.
Joice, William, labourer.

K

KELLY, David, clothes-dealer.
Kelter, Nanty, hostler.
Kingsborough, Robert, publican and chandler.

L

LAMB, William, hair-dresser.
Lee, John, guager.
Locke, John, blacksmith.

Long, James, reedmaker.
Leigh, William, surgeon and apothecary.
Lyons, William, publican.

M

Magennis, John, leather-cutter.
Magennis, Arthur, labourer.
Maguire, James, tailor.
Mallagh, Benjamin, surgeon and apothecary.
Mallagh, Margaret, huxter.
Mallon, John, nailer.
Manypeny, James, carpenter.
Marley, Roger, grocer and grain merchant.
Mathews, H. cooper.
Mathew, Henry, grocer.
Mathews, William, glazier.
May, William, watchmaker.
May, Thomas, delf merchant.
Midkiff, Joseph, wheelwright.
Mercer, Nicholas, whitesmith.
Miller, John and Co. grocers and leather-sellers.
Montgomery, Harford, baker.
Mooney, Charles, publican.
Morgan, John, huxter.
Morris, Patrick, huxter.
Morrison, Benjamin, shoemaker.
Morrison, Robert, tailor.
Morrow, George, farmer.
Morrow, Samuel, publican.
Mulholland, Patrick, carpenter.
Mulholland, Henry, carrier.
Mulholland, George, publican.

Mulholland, John, tailor.
Mulholland, John, boatman.
Murphy, Thomas, publican and woollen-draper.
Murphy, James, wheelwright.

Mᶜ

Mᶜ CANN, John, weaver.
Mᶜ Connell, Peter, farmer,
Mᶜ Connell, John, shoemaker.
Mᶜ Cullough, — hosier.
Mᶜ Court, John, labourer.
Mᶜ Grady, John, gardener.
Mᶜ Ildoon, John, labourer.
Mᶜ Kinley, William, saddler.
Mᶜ Murray, Robert, carrier.
Mᶜ Quiggan, James, huxter.

N

NEVILL, James, baker.

O

O'NEILL, B. C. schoolmaster.
Overend, William, merchant.
Overend, John, publican.

P

PAUL, William, haberdasher and woollen-draper.
Pettigrew, Mrs. Esther.

R

ROBB and JELLY, woollen-drapers.

Rogers, Christian, washwoman.
Rutledge, Rev. James.

S

SAUNDERSON, Henry M. surgeon and apothecary.
Saunderson, William, publican.
Saunderson, Hector, painter and glazier.
Saunderson, Elinor, haberdasher.
Scott, Andrew, cooper.
Sitherwood, John, watchmaker.
Shaw, George, carpenter.
Shillington, Thomas, grocer and grain merchant.
Sheppard, Martha, haberdasher.
Simons, John, mealmonger.
Sinnamon, Thomas, grocer and spirit merchant.
Stanley, Henry, grocer.
Stanton, John, slater.
Summerall, John, shoemaker.
Swean, William, weaver.
Sweaney, James, whitesmith.

T

THACKER, Thomas, carpenter.
Tracy, John, blacksmith.

W

WALKER, Joseph H. surgeon.
Williscroft, William, reedmaker.
Wilson, Thomas, woollen draper.
Woodhouse, Curran, Esq.
Woodhouse, John O. spirit merchant.
Woodhouse, George, publican.

Woodhouse, John, publican,
Wright, William, leather seller.
Wright, William, publican.
Wright, Joseph, shoemaker.
Wright, Thomas, huxter.

Historical Account of the Town of Tandragee.

TANDRAGEE, a market town in the county of Armagh, is situated eleven miles north of Newry, nine west from Armagh, seven and a half southwest from Lurgan, four south from Portadown, and about twenty-four south-west from Belfast.— It consists principally of one long and wide street, upon the south-eastern side of a hill, with a spacious market-place near the upper end. It is very beautifully situated, in a fine, populous and improved country—sheltered from the prevailing winds by fine trees, and almost surrounded by the picturesque and highly ornamented demense of Miss Sparrow, and that of the Rev. Dean Carter. On the top of the hill, there is a long and very handsome public walk, overshadowed by a row of the finest lime-trees in the kingdom. There is a very handsome church, surrounded by trees, finely situated on high ground, which deserves to be visited by travellers. It was built within these few years, on the site of an old church, which had become ruinous and too small for the congregation. The funds appropriated for its erection, having been unequal to its completion, it has very lately been finished at the sole expense of Miss Sparrow, the munificent proprietor of the town and large adjoining estate. It is a Gothic building, of great simplicity and elegance, with a high tower and pinnacles, which forms a beautiful object to the surrounding country. The interior is fitted up with singular taste; and on the whole, it is one of the handsomest and most convenient parish churches in the kingdom. In the centre of the town, there is also a neat and convenient Methodist chapel.

The mansion house, usually called the castle, is situate close to the town and church, upon the top of a steep bank, which commands a beautiful view of the romantic and finely wooded demesne. It was built some time ago, on the site of an old castle, formerly the residence of the chief of the sept of the O'Hanlons, and afterwards of the St. Johns, to the ancestor of whom, Lord Grandison, lord-deputy of Ireland, it was granted by Queen Elizabeth, and has, with the estates, descended to the present proprietor, Miss Sparrow—the only remaining representative of that ancient and illustrious family.—The river Cusier passes near the lower end of the town. It is a fine stream, and runs through beautiful wooded banks, from the Fews mountains, where it rises, until it falls into the river Bann, near Portadown; giving motion to a great number of mills and bleach works, and sending off, near the town, the principal supply to the Newry canal.

There has been, in addition to the fine ancient woods near the town, a very great number of new plantations made, which already are making a beautiful appearance. Miss Sparrow has lately built a very handsome school-house, for the education of thirty boys and thirty girls, to be supported entirely at her own expense—This building forms a fine object from many points of view. Near the town stands the glebe-house, at present occupied by the Rev. Thomas Carter, Dean of Tuam, and rector of the parish. It is finely situated on a bold eminence, and commands a delightful prospect. The country around Tandragee has been long celebrated for the manufacture of the best description of middle-priced yard wide linens in the kingdom, which are sold in the market, to a very large amount, every Wednesday. The market is one the largest in the county, and the weekly sales fall very little short of £7,000. The principal articles of trade are linens, yarn, butter, flax, flour and all sorts of provisions, with some cattle and pigs, and, in the season, a very great quantity of pork, which is mostly bought up for the Belfast and Newry markets.

Spacious as the street and market place is, it is thronged every Wednesday with such busy crowds as are astonishing to strangers; and the dealers frequenting it, are particularly commendable for their correctness and punctuality. There are four fairs in the year—on the 5th day of July and 5th of November, and on the first Wednesday in February and May, at which great number of horses and black cattle, &c. are disposed of. The Newry navigation passes within a mile of the town, and affords an easy conveyance, for weighty goods to and from Newry, and the country around Lough Neagh.

The post arrives daily at half-past eight o'clock in the morning, and is despatched at five in the afternoon.

The population of Tandragee amounts to about 1,200, of whom about two thirds are Protestants. The town contains a great number of well-supplied shops, and has been, for some years, increasing in business and respectability. The flax which is sold in this market, nearly to the amount of 2000 stones weekly, is reckoned the best in Ireland.

Directory of Tandragee, for 1819.

A

Abbott, William, blacksmith.
Acheson, James, diaper manufacturer and grocer.
Acheson, John, publican.
Adamson, John, publican.
Alcorn, Samuel, grocer.
Alexander, Hugh, grocer, hardware and delf merchant.
Allen, Mrs Letitia.
Allen, William, grocer and spirit-dealer.

B

Bailie, Joseph, carpenter.
Balance, John, publican.
Balmer, John, *Lodge*.
Baker, Thomas, stonecutter.
Barker, James, accountant.
Barnes, George, butcher.
Baxter, Robert, tinman.
Bell, John, whitesmith.
Best, Thomas, carpenter.
Best, John, carpenter.
Bisset, Thomas, breeches-maker.
Black, Saywell, shoemaker.
Bowers, William, hair-dresser.
Boyd, Robert, linen merchant.

Brewster, David, carpenter.
Burns, John, surgeon and apothecary.

C

Callen, John, mason.
Carter, Rev. Thomas, dean of Tuam and rector of Ballymore.
Clark, William, linen merchant, *Lark-hill.*
Conlon, Daniel, wheelwright.
Connor, Robert.
Courtney, Mary Anne, haberdasher.
Craig, George, publican and linen-buyer.
Creevy, John, Esq.
Creery, Rev. Leslie, rector of Kilmore and curate of
    Tandragee.
Crothers, Hugh, woollen-draper.
Culbert, J. schoolmaster.
Cupples, Mrs. *Prospect.*

D

Daily, Thomas, dealer.
Davis, James, draper.
Devin, Richard, yarn-dealer.
Dimm, John, publican.

E

Evans, Thomas, wheelwright.
Evans, John, carrier.
Evans, James, carpenter.

F

Farrell, James, dealer.

Fegan, Michael, blue-dier.
Feran, John, blacksmith.
Ferris, William, publican.
Flack, James, baker.
Flanagan, William, nailer.
Flanagan, George, nailer.
Foy, Daniel, grocer.

G

GAMBLE, James, grocer.
Gamble, William, manor constable.
Gibson, James, grocer.
Glenn, James, sawyer.
Glenn, Mary, huxter.
Gracy, Edward, spirit-dealer, and glass and china merchant.
Gracy, George, blacksmith.
Greenaway, Richard, publican.

H

HACKET, Mary, grocer.
Haddock, Anthony, linen merchant, *Mullahead*.
Haly, James, gent.
Haly, Patrick, brogue-maker.
Harden, Robert, Esq.
Hardy, George, grocer, spirit-dealer and hardware merchant.
Hardy, Abraham, publican, *Dog and Duck*.
Hardy, James, attorney.
Hardy, John, *Cooly-hill*.
Harford, Elizabeth, huxter.
Hood, Mrs. Isabella.
Hunter, William, hosier.
Hutchinson, William, wholesale spirit-dealer.

Hutchinson, John, innkeeper.
Hutchinson, David, woollendraper.

I

IVER, David, bookbinder.

J

JACKSON, John, grocery and seed-shop.
Johnson, Rev. William, probationary minister.
Joice, John, Esq. *Mullyavilly Lodge.*

K

KINKEAD, James, haberdasher.
Kinkead, Campbell, boot and shoemaker.
Kinnan, William, boot and shoemaker.
Kinnair, Alexander, tailor.

L

LARKIN, John, wheelwright.
Lake, Rev. John, *Mullavilly Glebe.*
Leigh, Thomas, Esq. *Clare Castle.*
Lennon, Felix, grocer and leather-seller.
Loftie, William, Esq.

M

MAGILL, James, woollendraper, grocer and spirit dealer.
Magennis, T. grocer.
Magennis, George, grocer.
Magennis, Sergeant.
Mains, Jeremiah, baker.
Mains, Elizabeth, publican.

Marks, William, grocer.
Mathews, Robert, painter and glazier.
Mathews, Margaret, haberdasher.
Meredith, William, carpenter.
Miller, William, shoemaker.
Montgomery, James, muslin and chequer manufacturer.
Montgomery, William, publican.
Montgomery, John, carpenter.
Moore, James, grocer.
Morrison, John, linen bleacher.
Murphy, Patrick, shoemaker.
Murray, George, sawyer.

M^c

M'AULEY, John, clock and watch-maker.
M'Bride, James, grocer.
M'Callan, Samuel, tallow chandler.
M'Cleland, Abraham, surgeon and apothecary.
M'Cleland, J. reedmaker.
M'Clure, Daniel, linen merchant, *Springfield*.
M'Connell, Corry, Esq. *Mullavilly*.
M'Connell, Richard, Esq. *Mullavilly*.
M'Connell, Patrick, land surveyor.
M'Connell, James, publican.
M'Connell, John, hair-dresser.
M'Connell, William, hair-desser.
M'Connell, Hugh, schoolmaster.
M'Creight, Andrew, Esq.
M'Cully, John, tailor.
M'Donnell, William, *Mullahead*.
M'Garvey, Partland, tailor.
M'Gaughy, Patrick, tailor.

M'Givern, James, publican.
M'Kell, James, grocer and spirit-dealer.
M'Kelvey, John, whitesmith.
M'Keown, William, brogue-maker.
M'Mahon, Charles, carrier.
M'Nally, John, butcher.
M'Nally, John, jun. butcher.
M'Night, John, carpenter.
M'Recker, Roland, teacher.

N

NEAL, Archibald, reedmaker.
Nelson, Jane, grocer.
Nelson, Robert, tallow chandler.

O

O'HANLON, John, publican.
O'Hara, Michael, tailor.
O'Neill, Henry, publican.

P

PATTON, George Washington, M. D.
Phelps, Joshua. *Broomfield.*
Prentice, Mrs. Mary.

Q

QUINN, William, publican.
Quinn, John, dealer.

R

RABB, Matthew, carpenter.

Rankin, John, shoemaker.
Rea, George, weaver.
Rice, John, linen bleacher, *Derryallen.*

S

SANDFORD, James, flax-dresser.
Saunderson, Francis, saddler and harness-maker.
Searight, John, diaper manufacturer, grocer, &c.
Sheppard, Parker, baker.
Skeffington, Hugh, leather-seller.
Stewart, John, reedmaker.
Summerville, Joseph, dealer.

T

TAGGART, James, gent.
Thompson, Thomas, *Bellfield.*
Tole, Mrs Mary.
Toner, William, nailer.
Topley, John, weaver.
Trotter, Robert & Richard, stamp and post-office, wholesale
    and retail grocers and spirit-dealers.
Trotter, West, slater.
Trouton, William, carpenter.

W

WHEALEY, Crawford, publican.
Whiteside, John, grocer.
Willis, John, grocer.
Wilson, Richard, publican.
Wilson, Samuel, weaver.

HISTORICAL ACCOUNT OF THE VILLAGE OF WARINGSTOWN.

THE village of Waringstown presents to the traveller a remarkably pleasing appearance. Timber of the largest growth—neat white washed cottages—the total absence of those heaps of filth, which so often disgrace the habitations of the lower orders in this country—and the general neatness and cleanliness of the place, render this one of the most agreeable villages in the kingdom.

At the north end of the village, a handsome house and demesne, belonging to John Brown, Esq. and, at the south, the residence of Mr. Thomas M'Murray, give a favourable impression at either entrance; and the mansion house* of the Waring family, which was built about the year 1667, by an ancestor of the present proprietor, is highly ornamental, having an ancient and respectable front, with extensive gardens and grounds, stored with forest trees, unequalled in this country for size and beauty. Near the house stands the parish church, embosomed in lofty trees. It is built in an antique and venerable style; has a very curious oak roof and a steeple of tolerable elevation. This church was erected before the commencement of the last century, by William Waring. Esq. at his sole expense, and presented to the parish.

---

* In the military events which preceded the battle of the Boyne, in 1698 this house was occupied alternately by the Irish army, and that of King William III. The Waring family were outlawed by King James, and forced to fly. The house then became a military depot of the Irish, and soon after, in the progress of the English array, Duke Schomberg took possession of it, and occupied it for some days, on his march towards the Boyne.

The linen trade, to which this part of the kingdom owes its prosperity and extremely dense population, first flourished in Lurgan and in this village; and the first diaper ever manufactured in Ireland, was woven here, by a colony from Lancashire, brought over soon after the revolution, by the then proprietor, Samuel Waring, Esq. M. P. one of the original institutors and members of the Linen Board. The neighbourhood of this village still continues a principal station of the diaper manufacture. Mr. John Brown and Sons deal very extensively in that branch, as also Mr. Richard Brown, and several others. Cambrick is also manufactured here, in the highest perfection, and on an extensive scale, by Mr. Thomas M'Murray, Mr. G. M'Murray, &c. &c. The finest web of cambrick ever produced in Ireland, having been made in this village, under the direction of Mr. T. M'Murray, was presented to her late majesty, Queen Charlotte. An excellent brewery and malt-house are established here by Mr. Robert Ruddock. A neat school-house, in which more than two hundred children are instructed on Sundays, by the benevolent care of the upper classes, is alike ornamental to the place, and creditable to its inhabitants. The population is supposed to exceed five hundred people, and the village has the appearance of unusual population, industry and comfort. Banbridge is the post-town; but in Waringstown there is a receiving-office, under the direction of the postmasters general.

Directory of Waringstown, for 1819.

A

ADAMSON, Robert, linen-draper, *Ballylough.*
Arnold, Edward, gent. *Perrymount.*
Atkinson, Valentine, gent. *Valentine Cottage.*

B

BAIRD, William, innkeeper.
Beatty, Robert, farmer, *Donaclony.*
Beatty, James, grocer and publican, *Donaclony.*
Black, John, farmer, *Mathers's Fort.*
Bleakley, David, gent. *Donaclony.*
Blizard, Conway, gent. *Moorfield.*
Brown, Joseph, gent. *Clare.*
Brown, Richard, merchant, *Diaper-hill.*
Brown, Joseph, merchant, *Brown bridge.*
Brown, John, linen and diaper manufacturer.
Brown, John and Co. diaper manufacturers.
Brown, Turner, grocer and spirit merchant.

C

CAGHEY, Aaron, bleacher.
Capper, Matthew, carpenter.
Carroll, William, shoemaker.

D

Daly, Dennis, butcher.
Denison, John, tailor.
Dougherty, Samuel, shoemaker.

F

Ferguson, John, grocer and diaper manufacturer, *Ballylough.*
Ferguson, Adam, diaper manufacturer, *Ballylough.*
Ferguson, James, diaper manufacturer, *Clare.*
Ferguson, George, diaper manufacturer, *Ballylough.*
Ferguson, Robert, diaper manufacturer, *Ballylough.*
Ferguson, Mary, diaper manufacturer, *Ballylough.*
Ferguson, Robert, surgeon and apothecary.
Forsythe, William, grocer.

K

Kennedy, James, blacksmith.
Kennedy, John, blacksmith.

L

Lindsay, James, publican, *Ballenabraget.*
Lunn, Edward, farmer, *Mathers's Fort.*
Lunn, Abraham, farmer, *Mathers's Fort.*

M

Manary, Samuel, cambrick manufacturer.
Manary, John, tailor.
Mills, Christopher, gent. *Bleary.*
Mills, William Richard and Co. diaper manufacturer, *Bleary.*
Moles, Oliver, diaper manufacturer, *Clare.*

Moles, Adam, gent.
Moorhead. John, innkeeper.
Morris, Thomas, constable.
Mullen, Daniel, nailer.
Murphy, John, shoemaker.

Mᶜ

M'Connell, John, wheelwright.
M'Connell, James, carpenter.
M'Cormick, Alexander, land steward to Mr. Waring.
M'Gowan, James, farmer, *Donaclony.*
M'Gowan, James, lime-burner, *Mathers's Fort.*
M'Kee, Dennis, butcher.
M'Keown, John, gent.
M'Keown, John. jun. gent.
M'Murray, George and Sons, linen merchants.
M'Murray, George, jun. merchant.
M'Stay, Francis, butcher.

N

New, John, gardener.
Nicholson, William, merchant, *Donaclony.*
Nicholson, George, merchant, *Ballywalter.*
Nicholson, James, merchant, *Ballywalter.*

Q

Quinn, Christopher, conservator, *Summer-hill.*
Quinn, Esther and Sons, grocers.

R

Richey, John, farmer, *Donaclony.*

Robinson, John, diaper manufacturer, *Donaclony.*
Ruddock, Robert, malster and brewer.

S

Scully, John, gent. *Corcrany.*
Shaw, William, merchant, *Holden's Valley.*
Sherrard, Rev. John, *Lamb's Island.*
Simpson, William, cooper.
Stevenson, John, farmer, *Castledoe.*
Stevenson, Patrick, shoemaker.
Stott, Rev. John, curate of Waringstown.

T

Turner, Edward, gent.

W

Waring, Rev. Holt, rector of Lurgan.
Waren, William, parish clerk and schoolmaster.

Historical Account of the Town of Lurgan.

Lurgan is situated about fourteen miles from Armagh, seventeen from Newry, and seventeen from Belfast. It is the second town in the county of Armagh, and was founded by William Brownlow, Esq. In 1619, it consisted of only forty-two houses, which were peopled with English families. The streets were paved, and kept remarkably clean, and two water-mills were constructed in the neighbourhood, for the benefit of the settlement. At present Lurgan is a beautiful town. It consists principally of one wide street, nearly a mile in length, and contains, at least, 379 houses, and 2207 inhabitants.

The church is spacious and well built, ornamented with a beautiful spire, and furnished with an excellent organ. There are also a commodious Presbyterian meeting-house, and a neat and comfortable Methodist chapel, at the rear of the beautiful residence of John Johnston, Esq.—A poor-school has been established here, which is supported by private subscriptions and an annual charity sermon. In this institution, nearly two hundred children receive education.

This town is situated in the extensive parish of Shankill, the rector of which (the Rev. Mr. Waring) receives his tithe by a *modus* of ten pence per acre, for which he agreed with his parishioners, and it is very cheerfully paid.

The trade of Lurgan consists chiefly in articles of the linen manufacture—viz. cambricks, lawns, diapers, and damasks; the sale of which, in the weekly market, averages from £2500 to £3000.

The beautiful and extensive demesne of Charles Brownlow,

Esq. adjoins the town. The mansion is a very antique castle, which has received many additions since it was originally built. The demesne is highly ornamented with rich plantations and a fine sheet of water, which is covered with every description of water fowl. A pleasant gravel walk surrounds the lake; and the demesne is always open for the amusement of the inhabitants.

Directory of Lurgan, for 1819.

A

ADAMS, William, tin-plate worker.
Allen, Thomas, teacher.
Armstrong, William, grocer and hardwareman.
Atkinson, William, spirit-dealer.

B

BARRETT, William, carrier, Pound river.
Beatty, Richard, grocer.
Bell, Robert, surgeon.
Bell, William, carpenter, Castle lane.
Bell, Elinor, grocer, *Ballyblough.*
Bell, Thomas, muslin manufacturer, *Ballyblough.*
Bell, John, clock and watch-maker.
Belshaw, Margaret, publican.
Becket, Leonard, carrier, Pound river.
Bingham, John, boot and shoemaker.
Bingham, Clements, boot and shoemaker.
Black, Jonathan, publican.
Black, Thomas, glass and earthenware dealer.
Black, Seywell, shoemaker.
Black, John, boot and shoemaker.
Black, Hugh, mason.
Boyd, James, brewer and tobacco manufacturer.
Boyland, Charles, hair-dresser.
Boyle, John, farmer, *Knocknashane.*
Brown, William, grocer and baker.

Brown, Youngston, publican, *Cross Keys.*
Brown, Sarah, dressmaker.
Brownlow, Charles, Esq. *Lurgan House.*
Brownlow, Charles, jun. Esq. M. P. *Lurgan House.*
Bullock, Moses, wheelwright and turner.
Bullock, Isaac, wheelwright and turner.
Bullock, Boyd, wheelwright and turner.
Bullock, Robert, grocer.
Bullock, Henry, huxter, Thomas street.
Bullock, Thomas, wheelwright.
Bullock, Thomas, shuttle and temple manufacturer.
Bullock, Nelson, farmer, Aughagallen road.
Bunteny, Thomas, weaver, Pound river.
Burke, William, solicitor.
Burns, Benjamin, weaver, *Ballyblough.*
Byrne, Thomas, gent. Castle lane.
Byrne, Ephraim, publican.
Byrne Michael, hostler, Pound river.

C

CALL, John, currier and leather-seller.
Campbell, Hugh, hosier.
Campbell, Catherine, haberdasher.
Carmichael, Henry, reedmaker, Pound river.
Carmichael, Esther, eating-house, Middle row.
Carnaghan, William, flaxdresser, Pound river.
Carroll, Philip, shoemaker.
Chapman, Richard, blacksmith.
Cherry, Samuel, carrier, Back lane.
Christy, Abel.
Christy, Robert, butcher.
Clendenning, John, coach wheel and farming utensil
    manufacturer.

Colven, Thomas, carpenter.
Colven, John, carpenter.
Colven, Henry, carpenter.
Cooper, John, spruce beer manufacturer,
Corr, Rosanna, grocer and spirit-dealer.
Corry, Peter, cooper.
Cubbage, Alexander, Esq. banker.
Cubbage, Mrs. Elizabeth.
Cunningham, Lucinda, innkeeper,

D

DARRAGH, William, grocer.
Dobbin, Mrs. Mary.
Donaldson, Francis, baker.
Donnelly, John, hawker.
Dougan, Bernard, grocer.
Dougan, Charles, huxter and lodging-house, *Ballyblogh*
   [*sic*].
Douglass, William, surgeon and apothecary.
Douglass, Henry, grocer, Thomas street.
Dowey, James, publican, Thomas street.
Druit, Joseph, linen merchant.
Druit, Thomas, linen merchant.

E

ECCLES, Nathaniel, hosier.
Emerson, George, tobacconist.
Emerson, William, pedlar.
Emerson, Thomas, pedlar.

F

FITZSIMMONS, James, spirit-dealer.
Fleming, Elizabeth, haberdasher.

Ford, Mrs. Ann.
Freil, Patrick, tobacco-spinner.
Fullon, Mary, publican, Castle lane.
Fullerton, William, nailer.

G

GIBSON, Thomas, shoemaker.
Gilbert, Anthony, farmer.
Gilbert, Henry, glass, china and earthenware-dealer.
Ginniff, Hugh, weaver.
Grainger, John, reedmaker, Thomas street.
Grant, Daniel, publican.
Greer, Samuel, Esq.
Greer, George, Esq.
Greer, Miss Jane,

H

HALFPENNY, Catherine, huxter.
Hall, Thomas, notary public and commissioner for taking
    affidavits.
Hall, Joseph, grocer.
Hamilton, Arthur, butcher.
Hamilton, James, butcher.
Hamilton, John, weaver, Castle lane.
Haslett, Mrs. Dorothy.
Hasleton, Robert, weaver.
Haughey, John, slater.
Hauton, Mrs. Hannah.
Heaney, John, slater, Back lane.
Henning, John, surgeon.
Henry, James, publican,
Henry, James, saddler, Middle row.
Hinds, Samuel, shoemaker.

Holywood, Job, shoemaker, *Ballyblough*.
Hughes, Thomas, linendraper, publican and grocer.
Hughes, Edward, baker.
Hurst, Thomas, taylor.

I

IRWIN, Martha, haberdasher.

J

JENKINSON, Thomas, wheelwright.
Johnston, Thomas, gent.
Johnston, John, brewer.
Johnston, James, proprietor of the Armagh coach.
Johnston, Edward, publican.
Johnston, William, spirit merchant.
Johnston, William, grocer.
Johnston, Samuel, warehouseman, Castle lane.
Johnston, William, shoemaker, Thomas street.
Jordan, Samuel, malt-maker.

K

KELLY, Rev. John, P. P.
Kelly, Arthur, shuttle-maker.
Kennedy, Edward, linen merchant.
Kennedy, Richard, weaver.
Kennedy, John, blacksmith.
Kennedy, James, copper and tin-plate worker.
Kerr, William, soap-boiler and tallow chandler.
Kerr, Mary, haberdasher and straw bonnet-maker.
Kirk, Samuel, soap-boiler and tallow chandler.
Kinny, Alexander, carpenter.

L

LANGTRY, William, farmer, *Cherrymount.*
Langtry, Samuel, shoemaker.
Lappan, Henry, butcher.
Lawson, Alexander, hatter.
Lenaghan, Daniel, blacksmith.
Leonard, Sames, sergeant.
Lewis, James, shoemaker.
Lynas, William, shoemaker.

M

MAGEE, M. M. gent.
Magee, John, weaver.
Magee, Thomas, saddler, Middle row.
Mahaffy, John, shoemaker.
Mahaffy, Mary, mantua-maker.
Malcom, Thomas, woollendraper.
Malcomson, Joseph, Esq. banker.
Martin, Patrick, gardener.
Maxwell, Arrabella, woollendraper.
Melvin, Henry, huxster.
Mercer, Duke, butcher.
Mills, James, publican.
Millhouse, Thomas.
Moffet, Robert, shoemaker.
Monroe, William, saddler and harness-maker.
Montgomery, Hugh, lodging-house.
Moore, Sampson, linen merchant.
Moore, James, huxter.
Morris, Ann, post-mistress and woollendraper.
Morrow, William, shoemaker.
Murphy, James, publican.

Murtagh, James, publican.

Mᶜ

M'ALISTER, Luke.
M'Cabe, Edward, painter and glazier.
M'Clean, Edward, weaver.
M'Colm, Alexander, nailer.
M'Combs, John, publican.
M'Combs, John, carpenter.
M'Cullough, William, grocer and tallow chandler.
M'Gowan, James.
M'Gowan, George, weaver.
M'Gowan, Andrew, carpenter.
M'Grady, Bernard, barrack-master.
M'Kelvy, Robert, shoemaker.
M'Kenna, Richardson, tailor.
M'Kenna, Sarah, huxter.
M'Keown, William, grocer and timber merchant.
M'Mullen, John, nailer.
M'Murray, Robert, publican.
M'Neill, Richard, weaver.
M'Veigh, Henry, Esq. banker.

N

NETTLETON, George.
Nettleton, Ellen, grocer and spirit dealer.
Newbury, Dawson, publican.

O

OLDFIELD, Rev. John, curate of Lurgan.
O'Neill, Henry, weaver.
Orr, Thomas, guager.
Orr, John, shoemaker.

Overend, Misses.
Owens, Francis, butcher.

P

PENTLAND, John, tanner.
Pinchon, Jane, grocer.
Pollock, Alexander, barber.
Porter, Henry, clothes-dealer.

R

RANDLES, Michael, tailor.
Reilly, Robert, shoemaker.
Richardson, Mrs. Lucy.
Ridgeway, Thomas, shoemaker.
Ridgeway, Richard, shoemaker.
Ridgeway, Henry, shoemaker.
Roberts, Alexander, ladies' shoemaker.
Roberts, Robert, shoemaker.
Robson, Thomas, grocer.
Robson, Elizabeth, grocer.
Rodgers, Samuel, shoemaker.
Ross, William, publican.
Ruddle, James, publican,
Russell, Valentine, publican.

S

SAVAGE, Robert, grocer and tallow chandler.
Savage, Henry, hatter.
Shannon, Peter, publican.
Shaw, Robert, grocer and spirit-dealer.
Sheppard, James, weaver.
Smart, David, innkeeper.

Smith, William, baker.
Stanhope, Hamilton, tailor.
Stuart, Colonel.
Swain, Joseph, gardener.

T

TAAFE, John, carpenter.
Taylor, Samuel, schoolmaster.
Thompson, David, publican and carman's inn.
Thompson, John, reedmaker.
Thompson, John, carpenter and shuttle-maker.
Thornberry, William, shoemaker.
Todd, Richard J. general auctioneer.
Torrington, Andrew, house and coach painter.
Trail, Robert, woollendraper.
Turkington, David, farmer.
Turkington, James, publican, *Duke of York.*
Twineham, James, weaver.

W

WARES, Thomas, teacher.
Watson, Francis, linen merchant.
Watson, Robert, diaper manufacturer.
Watt, William, publican.
Weatherall, William, shoemaker.
Wells, Matthew, clock and watchmaker.
White, John, gardener.
Whittle, Elizabeth, spirit-dealer.
Wilson, Mary, woollendraper.
Wilson, Jane.

Y

YOUNG, James, painter and glazier.

DIRECTORY OF BANBRIDGE, FOR 1819.

A

ADAIR, Robert, horse-dealer.
Amberson, James, schoolmaster.
Amberson, Samuel, publican.
Anderson, George, grocer.
Anderson, Joseph, shoemaker.
Anderson, John, shoemaker.
Anderson, Thomas, publican.
Ardray, William, publican,
Ardray, Robert, publican and butter merchant.
Armour, James, carpenter.
Arthurs, Mary, grocer.

B

BANEN, — surgeon.
Beatty, Rev. Thomas, *Vicarage.*
Bell, Mrs. Mary.
Bell, John, publican and grocer.
Black, George.
Blizard, John, Esq. *Bannview.*
Boyle, Mrs. innkeeper, *Devonshire Arms.*
Bradford, John, gent.
Bradford, Robert, cooper.
Bradford, Robert, house of entertainment.
Brownlow, Hugh, grocer.

Bryson, Samuel, hostler.
Buckley, Bernard, publican.
Byrne, Hugh, publican.
Byrne, Hugh, tailor.
Byrne, John, tailor.
Byrne, P. C. Esq. *Ardbien*.
Byrne, Thomas, paver.

C

CAMPBELL, John, house of entertainment.
Campbell, Samuel, victualler.
Campbell, Samuel, victualler.
Campbell, James, victualler.
Card, James, cart and plough-maker.
Card, William, cart and plough-maker.
Cleborn, Edward, linen and flour merchant.
Christy, James, Esq. *Lawrencetown House*.
Closs, James, house of entertainment.
Cochran, James, Esq. *Coushill*.
Craig, Mary, haberdasher.
Crawford, George, Esq. *Ballyeivy*.
Crawford, Andrew, Esq. *Milltown*.
Crawford, Walter, Esq. *Ballyeivy House*.
Creily, James, plasterer,
Crothers and Henry, haberdashers.
Crozier, George, solicitor.
Crozier, Thomas, solicitor.

D

DAVIS, Rev. James, *Henry-hill*.
Dickson, John.
Degney, Bridget, fruit-seller.

Douglas, Hugh, house of entertainment.
Downes, Thomas, shoemaker.
Downes, Norton, shoemaker.
Downes, Robert, publican and shoemaker.
Drennen, Samuel, victualler.
Dunbar, Hugh, grocer.

E

EDMONSON, Joseph, brick-maker.
Evans, John, wheelwright.
Evans, Robert, shoemaker.
Evans, William, sawyer.

F

FAIR, Alexander, mail coach agent.
Farrell, — surgeon.
Finley, John, grocery and spirit stores.
Flanagan, William, lock and gunsmith.
Fowler, James, Esq. *Bannville.*
Frazer, Hugh, attorney.
Frazer, David, blacksmith.

G

GARDNER, Thomas, linen merchant.
Gibson, Andrew, labourer.
Gilmore and Chapman, merchants.
Glass, Samuel, grocer.
Glass, John, slater.
Gorman, Patrick, house of entertainment.
Graham, Samuel, hide merchant.
Gribbon, John.

H

HAMILTON, Maxwell, publican.
Hawthorn, George, M. D.
Hayes, William, Esq. *Millmount.*
Heron, John, grocer.
Hopkins, Andrew, wheelwright.
Hosack, Hannah, publican.
Hudson, William, Esq. *Ballydown.*
Hughes, Patrick, linguist.
Hughes, Patrick, blacksmith.
Hutchinson, Thomas, painter, blue dier and grocer.

J

JOHNSON, Rev. John, master of the academy.
Johnson, James, taylor [*sic*].
Joice, Esther, publican.

K

KEARNS, Philip, baker.
Kelly, Robert, shuttle-maker.
Kelly, Misses, dress-makers.
Kelly, Robert, Esq. *Eliza-hill.*
Kenear, John, grocer and leather-seller.
Kennedy, Hugh, mason.
Kerr, Hamilton, publican.
Kirk, William, carter.

L

LAVERY, John, grocer and leather-seller.
Lawson, Rachael, haberdasher.
Law, Samuel, Esq. *Hazle-bank.*

Law, Joseph, Esq. *Cousville.*
Leech, — painter and glazier.
Lindsay, Elizabeth, fruit-seller.
Little, — surgeon.
Little, Andrew, brushmaker.
Little, Mrs. *Roseville.*
Locke, John, house of entertainment.
Love, John, grocer.
Lowry, Alexander, Esq. *Linen-hill.*

M

MACKLIN, Thomas, grocer.
Magee, Dudley, bailiff.
Magill, John, publican.
Main, John, woollendraper.
Major, Mrs. China, delf, and glass warehouse.
Mackin, Patrick, house of entertainment.
Malcomson, — surgeon.
Matier, Hugh, wheelwright.
Merren, William, postmaster.
Mitchell, Henry, joiner.
Mitchell, James, painter and glazier.
Moore, William and James, nursery and seed merchants.
Moore, Matthew, publican.
Moore, Thomas, publican.
Moorhead, Thomas, publican.
Morron, James, victualler.
Morron, John, victualler.
Morton, George, publican.
Morton, Joseph, publican.
Morton, Andrew, grocer.
Morton, Misses, milliners.

Mullen, Daniel, gent.
Mulligan, Gilbert, Esq. *Ballyeivy.*
Mulligan, John, Esq. *Parkmount.*
Mulligan, James, Esq. *Charleville.*
Mulligan, John, Esq. *Tullyconnaught.*
Mulligan, Hugh, grocer.
Munn, James, joiner.

Mᶜ

Mᶜ'ALINDEN, Henry, cabinet warehouse.
Mᶜ'Alinden, John, carter.
Mᶜ'Alister, Robert, shoemaker.
Mᶜ'Bride, Hugh.
Mᶜ'Campton, Daniel, tailor.
Mᶜ'Cariston, James, grocer.
Mᶜ'Clelland, Andrew, woollendraper.
Mᶜ'Clelland, John, Esq. *Gospelville.*
Mᶜ'Clelland, William, haberdasher.
Mᶜ'Clelland, Samuel, publican.
Mᶜ'Clelland, Robert, china and delf merchant.
Mᶜ'Clelland, John, hosiery and shoe shop.
Mᶜ'Clelland, Thomas, china and delf warehouse.
Mᶜ'Clelland, Thomas, bailiff.
Mᶜ'Connell, Charles, publican.
Mᶜ'Cormick, Robert, saddler.
Mᶜ'Creight, Rev. James, *Seapatrick Glebe.*
Mᶜ'Crory, David, publican.
Mᶜ'Crumb, John, tailor.
Mᶜ'Donald, John, chandler.
Mᶜ'Donald, John, cooper.
Mᶜ'Donald, John, tobacco-spinner.
Mᶜ'Fadden, Hugh, gent.

M'Garry, Hamilton, grocer, baker and spirit-dealer.
M'Grath, James, publican.
M'Kinstry, William, sawyer.
M'Mordie, Hans, Esq. *Bannview.*
M'Mordie, John, hosier.
M'Tair, James, nailer.
M'Williams, William, merchant.
M'Williams, Mrs.
M'Williams. Robert, grocer.
M'Williams, James, publican.
M'Williams, Ann.

N

NEILL, Robert, shoemaker.
Nelson, Joseph, watchmaker and jeweller.
Nelson, James, watchmaker.
Nelson, Mrs. Ann.

O

O'FLAGHERTY, F. grocer and seed merchant.
O'Neill, John, cabinet-maker and upholsterer.
O'Neill, David, turnpike gate-keeper.

P

PARKER, Henry, sexton.
Parker, John, nailer.
Pentland, James, grocer.
Pettigrew, William, Esq. *Lenaderg House.*
Potts, Richard, publican, delf and glass warehouse.

Q

QUINN, Daniel, grocer, soap-boiler, chandler and tobacconist.

R

RANKIN, Nathaniel, blacksmith.
Raw, Patrick, confectioner.
Reid, John, musician and dancing-master.
Ross, Robert, yarn merchant.
Rotley, Daniel.
Rutherford, Rev. John, *Elizaville.*

S

SALTS, Robert, publican.
Saunderson, — surgeon.
Savage, William, nursery and seeds-man.
Scott, John, woollendraper.
Scott, Robert, grocer, baker and spirit-dealer.
Scott, William, publican.
Scott, James, victualler.
Scriven, Captain, *Ballymony Lodge.*
Searight, Mrs.
Sergeant, — shuttle-maker.
Shannon, James, haberdasher.
Shields, James, teacher of the Lancasterian school.
Sloan, James, grocer.
Sloan, Miss, confectioner.
Steel, James, grocer and soap-boiler.
Spence, William, Esq. *Ballygowan Lodge.*

T

TITTERINGTON, Matthew, house of entertainment.

W

WALLACE, William, sawyer.
Waugh, John, Esq. *Whitehill.*
Weathers, James, mathematician.
Wier, Jane, grocery and spirit store.
Wier, Mr. William, *Lenaderg.*
Wier, Hugh, tailor.
White, George, grocer and publican.
White, Richard, baker.
Willis, William, house of entertainment. Wilson, James.
Woods, Moses, *Ballyvarley House.*
Woods, James, *Ballyvarley House.*
Woods, Moses, solicitor,
Woods, John, grocer, spirit and hardware merchant.
Wright, Samuel, carter.

HISTORICAL ACCOUNT OF THE
TOWN OF DUNGANNON.

D UNGANNON, in the county of Tyrone, is situated in latitude 54° 38′ north, and longitude 6° 39′ west, and stands on the south and western declivity of a high hill, on the summit of which stood an old castle, said to be built by the O'Nials, the then proprietors, and chiefs of Ulster.

Dungannon appears to have been a very ancient place. In the reign of James I. letters patent were issued to the Chichester family, granting to them and their heirs for ever, the manor of Dungannon, with many privileges rarely given to manors in those days. The seneschal is invested with full power to issue his attachment, to arrest either body or goods, for the recovery of debts contracted in said manor, to any amount under £20.

Immediately after granting those letters patent, Dungannon appears to have been increasing in trade and population; and, in consequence of the loyalty of its inhabitants, and their attachment to the laws of the country, letters patent were also granted, appointing Dungannon a borough, governed by a portrieve (or provost) and twelve burgesses, and directing them, to elect two honest, sober, and discreet men, to represent them in Parliament.

When the union took place between the two countries, the number of commoners being reduced, Dungannon was put in nomination for that purpose; but, fortunately, it was able to sustain its former dignity, and at present returns a member to the Imperial Parliament.

The ancestors of the present landlord, Lord Viscount Northland, possessed the old castle for ages, until its mouldering walls began to shew symptoms of decay. The family then removed to the mansion built by the late Lord Northland, at Dungannon Park. On the site of the old castle, T. K. Hannington, Esq. about the year 1790, erected a handsome castle, in the modern style. Being on the highest part of the hill, it affords a pleasing prospect of the adjoining country.

About the year 1750, under the fostering hand of the late Lord Northland, Dungannon began to shew a new and better appearance. At that time, the houses were built with stone, and covered with shingles or straw, and consisted of four streets. At present the town is nearly rebuilt, and widely extended. About the year 1790, the present Lord Northland formed a number of new streets, on the western side of the town, commonly known by the name of the New Town, which, since that period, has improved beyond expectation.

Dungannon, it appears, was the seat of a seminary of learning, by some called a priory, which stood in the suburbs, in a place called *Anna Ballysegart*,* where some foundations, and many pieces of stones, have been dug up. It appears to have been built in the Gothic order.

The parish church stands nearly in the centre of the town, and is a handsome modern building. The tower and spire was finished a few years ago, at the expense of the late Lord Northland, who also made the inhabitants a present of an excellent town clock.—The Rev. William Ball is the present rector of the parish.

In Dungannon there is also a Presbyterian meeting-house, a Roman Catholic chapel, and two Methodist preaching-houses. At the head of George's-street stands a baronial gaol and a courthouse, both of which have been lately erected.

The principal market of Dungannon is held on Thursday, and in it almost every article in common use is bought and sold.

---

* The town of priests.

Brown linen, seven-eighths wide, forms a principal article of commerce. By a report from the secretary of the Linen Board, in 1816, this appears to be one of the most considerable linen markets in Ireland. It has been ascertained that about £4000 is laid out weekly in this market, in that kind of fabrick.

A market is held every Monday for the sale of grain, particularly oats, which has of late been, very considerable. In September, 1818, there was sold, in one day, upwards of eight hundred sacks. A few years ago, there was erected, in William-street, a Market-house for the convenience of the grain trade. In 1814, a yarn-hall was also erected at the corner of William-street and George's-street, which has been of considerable service to that branch of our staple manufacture.

A market for the sale of cattle was commenced on Thursday the 5th of August last, custom free, which will be continued on the first Thursday in every month.

A Fever Hospital was established in Charles-street, supported by subscriptions, which has been of great service to the poorer classes of society. Fortunately for the community at large, there has been no applications for admission, for some time past.—In 1816, a Dispensary was also established, under the superintendance of Surgeon Sinclair.

In the vicinity of the town, there has lately been erected, a very extensive and convenient distillery, and also a brewery; they are at present in full work.

In Northland-row, there is an academy or charter-shool, for the education of a number of boys. The Rev. Dr. Dowdall is the present principal.—A school for the education of poor children has also been established on the foundation of the late Erasmus Smith; and another, for the education of females, is supported by Lady Northland. There is also a Sunday-school.

In September, 1819, a Savings Bank was instituted, at the expense and under the patronage of Lord Northland.

Dungannon is well supplied with coals from the neighbouring pits, and turbary from the adjacent country, at moderate prices.—A fountain erected in William-street, by the present Lord Northland, affords the inhabitants an abundant supply of good spring water.

By a census taken a few years ago, it appears the population of Dungannon consisted of 4000 persons; latterly it seems to have increased.

Dungannon is memorable for three important meetings. The first was held on the 15th of Feb. 1782. On that day, representatives from one hundred and forty-three Volunteer corps attended, and entered into resolutions which produced for Ireland the most beneficial results. The second was held on 8th of September, 1783. This meeting was attended by the most respectable characters in Ulster. Their resolutions, expressing the general principles of a proposed reform in Parliament, were passed unanimously. The third meeting was held in February, 1793, and was composed of delegates from every county in Ulster. The then government was so alarmed at their resolutions that the Convention Bill was enacted to put a stop to such meetings.

Directory of Dungannon, for 1819.

A

Agnew, Joseph, huxter, Church street.
Alexander, J. teacher, Perry street.
Anderson, Thomas, Capt. R. M. Anderson place.
Anderson, James, gent. Anderson place.
Anderson, Alexander, publican, Scotch street.
Anderson, William, gardener, *Milltown*.
Anderson, James, gardener, *Milltown*.
Atwell, William, shoemaker, Ann street.

B

Barclay, Robert, Esq. Market street.
Barton, John, huxter, Irish street.
Bailie, Samuel, hatter, Carr's row.
Beatty, John, soap-boiler and tallow chandler, Scotch street.
Beavers, John, publican and butcher, Irish street.
Begley, John, huxter, Irish street.
Bell, Miss Mary, Market street.
Bell, William, painter and glazier, Scotch street.
Bennett, Rev. David, Scotch street.
Blakely, Mrs. Ann, Ann street.
Boardman, Thomas, bleacher, *Moygashell*.
Boardman, Thomas, *Laurel-hill*.
Bourne, Rev. Sandford, *Glebe-hill*.
Branagan, Francis, grocer and publican.

Brawley, J. reedmaker.

Brennan, Miss, china and delf shop, Scotch street.

Briton, Thomas, sawyer, Perry street.

Brown, Nicholas, Esq. Market street.

Brown, Robert, Esq. Scotch street.

Brown, James, Esq. *Beech Valley.*

Brown, David, linendraper, grocer, tallow chandler and baker, *Donaghmore.*

Brownlee, John, constable, Perry street.

Bullock, Ann, seminary for young ladies, George's street.

Buntin, John, dealer, *Milltown.*

Burrows, John, leather merchant, Market street.

Byrne, Luke, coppersmith, Perry street.

C

CALLAGHAN, Owen, leather merchant, Irish st.

Campbell, Edward, huxter, Scotch street.

Canning, William, printer of the *Ulster Chronicle,* Market street.

Carpendale, Rev. Thomas, *Killyman.*

Carroll, John, carrier, Scotch street.

Carson, William, baker, Perry street.

Cassiday, John, hair-dresser, Church street.

Cavanagh, Bernard, cooper, Perry street.

Cavanagh, Patrick, cooper, Church street.

Charleston, Margaret, huxter, New Town.

Chichester, Charles, clock and watchmaker, Church street.

Clarke, James, grocer, Irish street.

Clarke, Mrs. grocer, Scotch street.

Clarke, George, shoemaker, Perry street.

Clarke, James, brogue-maker, Carr's row.

Conway, Michael, cooper, School lane.

Conwell, Rev. Henry, Ann street.

Conwell, Rev. Daniel, P. P. *Donaghmore.*

Cooper, J. agent to the distillery, *Milltown.*

Coote, Robert, stationer and woollendraper, Market street.

Copeland, Robert, huxter, New Town.

Corr, James, mason, Irish street.

Corran, — auctioneer, Scotch street.

Corry, James, carpenter, Sloan street.

Crump, Joshua, Esq. Northland row.

Cullen, James, carpenter, Ann street.

Cunningham, John, huxter, Irish street.

D

DALY, William, carrier, Carr's row.

Daly, John, carrier, Carr's row.

Davidson, Samuel, solicitor, School-house lane.

Davidson, George, whitesmith, Perry street.

Davidson, Robert, blue-dier, Irish street.

Dawson, William, surgeon and apothecary, Scotch street.

Dawson, Thomas, grocer, Scotch street.

D'Acosta, Monsieur, teacher of French language, Perry street.

Devlin, Patrick, publican, Church street.

Dickson, Benjamin, surgeon and apothecary, Market street.

Dickson, David, woollendraper.

Dickson, John, M. D. Northland row.

Dickson, David, saddler and harness-maker, Scotch street.

Dickson, John, surgeon, school-house lane.

Dickson, Mrs. Gustavus, George's street.

Dilworth, Messrs, grocers. Church street.

Doak, William, painter and glazier, Church street.

Donaldson, Mrs. George's street.

Donnelly, Bernard, publican, *Donaghmore.*
Donnelly, Daniel, mason, Church street.
Douglass, Francis, ladies' shoemaker, Perry street.
Dowdall, Rev. Dr. college.
Dowse, Richard, surgeon and apothecary, Church street.
Dowse, Richard, gent. George's street.
Duffy, Alexander, architect, *Milltown.*

E

Evans, Edward, Esq.
Evans, Rev. Robert, Perry street.

F

Falls, John, distillery.
Falls, Richard, excise officer, George's street.
Feney, Patrick, publican, Market street.
Fegan, Owen, huxter, Irish street.
Ferguson, James, Esq.
Ferguson, Patrick, Esq. *Lisdermott.*
Fox, Hugh, publican, Church street.
Fox, Daniel, publican, Church street.
Fox, Luke, publican, Scotch street.
Fox, Bernard, publican, Irish street.
Fox, — huxter, Scotch street.
Frizell, Alexander, grocer, Church street.
Frizell, Richard, blue-dier, Scotch street.
Frizell, John, nailer, Irish street.
Frizell, Lewis, clock and watchmaker, Irish street.
Frizell, Robert, nailer, George's street.
Frizell, Robert, town-sergeant, Perry street.
Fullan, Arthur, commissioner for taking affidavits, Market
    street.

G

GAITENS, William, carpenter, William street.
Galbraith, Misses, Scotch street.
Geraghty, Thomas, Esq. brewer; house, Northland row.
Geraghty, Thomas, wheelwright, Market street.
Garratt, William, *Torren-hill.*
Ginn, George, painter and glazier, Scotch street.
Girvan, William, distiller, *Milltown.*
Glass, Alexander, grocer, Scotch street.
Glass, Miss Martha, George's street.
Glass, Robert, gent. George's street.
Graham, Rev. James, *Thorn-hill.*
Gray, John, watchmaker, Church street.
Gray, James, coppersmith, Scotch street.
Graves, Messrs. Northland row.
Greeves, John, grocer, Perry street.
Greeves, Thomas, haberdasher, Perry street.
Green, George, nailer, Church street.
Green, John, nailer, Perry street.
Greer, Thomas, Esq. *Rhone-hill.*
Grey, William, Esq. *Milltown.*
Greer, Thomas, Esq. *Newhamburgh.*
Greer, Joseph, gent. Irish street.

H

HADDOCK, Joseph, tailor, Scotch street.
Hagerty, Patrick, dealer in flax.
Hall, James, publican, *Waterloo Tavern,* Irish st.
Halyday, Reuben, cabinet-maker and upholsterer, William
    street.
Hamilton, Thomas, surgeon and apothecary, Market street.
Hamilton, James, shoemaker, Ann street.

Hancock, James, soap-boiler and chandler, Irish st.

Hancock, Robert, publican, Scotch street.

Hanna, Misses, haberdashers, Market street.

Hannington, Thomas, Esq. *Knox Castle.*

Hansley, Patrick, teacher of Erasmus Smith's school.

Harker, Francis, teacher, Scotch street.

Hart, William, innkeeper, *Verner's-bridge.*

Haughey, H. huxter, Irish street.

Heathers, James, woollendraper, Market street.

Heathers, William, woollendraper and haberdasher, Market street.

Heburn, Michael, clothes-dealer, Irish street.

Henderson, Richard, whitesmith, Perry street.

Higgins, Samuel, Esq. Market street.

Hodgett, Thomas, nailer, Ann street.

Hogg, Rev. James, *Carton.*

Holmes, William, solicitor, Scotch street.

Hughes, John, postmaster, Market street.

Hughes, Patrick, baker, Market street.

Hughes, Edward, leather merchant, Irish street.

Hugo, Arthur, Esq. surveyor of excise, *Milltown.*

Hurst, Henry, carpenter, Scotch street.

I

Irwin, T. M. Esq. *Drumglass House.*

Irwin, Joseph, saddler and harness-maker, Irish st.

J

Johnston, Charles, publican, Market street.

K

Kavanagh, — cooper, Irish street.

Kelly, James, publican, Irish street.

Kelly, Matthew, bookbinder, *Milltown.*

Kelly, Jonathan, weigh-master, William street.

Kierney, Richard, nailer, Ann street.

Kennedy, Charles, mealmonger, Ann street.

Kennedy, Charles, blacksmith, Church street.

King, Samuel, soap-boiler and tallow chandler, Market street.

King, Samuel, gent. *Moygashall.*

King, Robert, woollendraper, grocer and rope manufacturer, Market street.

Knox, Hon. Vesey, *Bernagh.*

Kyle, John, dealer, Scotch street.

L

Larkin, Thomas, publican, Perry street.

Lavel, Cornelius, M. D. High street.

Lavery, Patrick, huxter, Irish street.

Lelburn, Thomas, joiner and builder, Scotch st.

Loftus, Charles, painter and glazier, Irish street.

Loughran, Patrick, publican, Scotch street.

Loughran, Patrick, huxter, Irish street.

Lloyd, Richard, Esq. *Tamnamore.*

Lloyd, Jackson, Esq. *Killyman.*

Lowry, Theophilus, surgeon & apothecary, Scotch street.

Lowry, James, deputy weigh-master, Shambles lane.

Lyons, Mrs. Scotch street.

Lyster, Mary Ann, china and delf shop, Irish st.

Ludlow, Richard, agent, Perry street.

Lutton, Robert, blacksmith and farrier, George's street.

M

Mackenzie, Alexander, discount office, Market street.

Mackenzie, Alex. Esq. spirit store and brewery.

Maguire, John, nailer, Scotch street.

Maguire, Patrick, whitesmith, Perry street.

Mallon, Arthur, haberdasher, Church street.

Maxwell, Mrs. Perry street.

Meenagh, John, carpenter, Perry street.

Meenin, Owen, carrier, Shambles lane.

Moran, Mrs. confectioner, Church street.

Moorhead, William, saddler and harness-maker, Market street.

Morrow, James, grocer, Market street.

Morrow, George, leather-cutter, Sloan street.

Morrow, Samuel, grocer and woollendraper, *Carton.*

Mulgrew, Edward, publican, Church street.

Mullan, James, publican, Scotch street.

Mullan, John, grocer, Scotch street.

Mullan, Thomas, clock & watch-maker, Scotch st.

Mullan, John, wheelwright and turner, Irish street.

Mullan, James, tailor, New Town.

Mullan, John, butcher, Shamble lane.

Murphy, — nailer, Irish street.

Murphy, J. and P. carriers, Perry street.

Murray, Rev. Samuel.

Murray, William, Esq. sovereign and seneschal.

Murray, James, Esq. *Bloomhill.*

Murray, J. S. Esq. *Torren Mount.*

Murray, Rev. Richard, *Brackaville.*

M^c

M'Alinden, Felix, huxter, Perry street.

M'Anally, Francis, baker, Irish street.

M'Anally, Mrs. reedmaker, Irish street.

M'Avoy, John, Esq. *Bellmount.*

M'Avoy, William, spirit merchant, Church street.

M'Avoy, John, travelling jeweller, Irish street.

M'Can, Robert, cooper.

M'Cartney, John, sawyer, William street.

M'Cartney, William, carpenter, Perry street.

M'Clean, William, surgeon, Irish street.

M'Clelland, Ledford, soap-boiler and chandler, Market
    street.

M'Clelland, James, grocer, Irish street.

M'Court, — publican, Shamble lane.

M'Court, Daniel, plasterer, George's street.

M'Elnew, — publican, Church street.

M'Elhone, B. & D, butchers, Irish street.

M'Ginn, — farmer, Perry street.

M'Grath, George, dancing-master, Ann street.

M'Gubby, William, confectioner, William street.

M'Guffin, John, shoemaker, Ann street.

M'Guffin, Robert, shoemaker, Ann street.

M'Guigan, Neal, meal merchant, Irish street.

M'Ilroy, John, woollendraper and haberdasher, Market
    street.

M'Ilroy, William, gent. Tempin row, *Killyman.*

M'Iver, Matthias, M. D. Irish street.

M'Ilvogue, J. publican, Market street.

M'Kagney, Joseph, skinner, Irish street.

M'Kaghey, John, skinner, Ann street.

M'Kinley, Francis, wheelwright and turner, Irish street.

M'Kinny, Francis, teacher, Scotch street.

M'Mahan, Peter, tailor, *Milltown.*

M'Minn, Alexander, Publican, Irish street.

M'Namara, John, attorney's clerk.

M'Niece, Samuel, saddler and publican, Irish st.

M'Neill, H. E. Esq. *Killyneal.*
M'Randles, Oliver, dealer, Perry street.
M'Shane, Charles, teacher, Scotch street.
M'Shane, Owen, tailor, Scotch street.
M'Shane, Patrick, carpenter, Irish street.
M'Shane, Roger, mason, Irish street.
M'Shane, Bernard, mason, Irish street.
M'Shane, — huxter, Irish street.

N

NEVIL, James, boot and shoemaker, Irish street.
Nevil, James, shoemaker, Irish street.
Nevins, J. carpenter, &c. George's street.
Newburn, — hosier, Irish street.
Newton, Andrew, solicitor, Scotch street.
Northland, Right Hon. Lord Vicount, *Northland House.*

O

O'FARRELL, Francis, teacher, George's street.
Ogle, James, grocer, ironmonger, soap-boiler and chandler, Market street.
O'Neill, Felix, mathematician, George's street.
O'Neill, Constantine, hatter, Ann street.

P

PEARCE, John, tailor, Church street.
Peebles, Kinley and Deale, wholesale and retail grocers, and spirit merchants, Market street.
Peebles & Kinley, woollendrapers and haberdashers, Market street.
Phenix, Thomas, linendraper, Ann street.
Pike, William, Esq. *Derryvale.*

Pike, Jonathan, Esq. *Beechgrove.*
Preston, Patrick, baker, Market street.
Prunty, Edward, carrier, Irish street.

Q

Quin, W. J. Esq. solicitor, Northland row.
Quin, Charles, publican, Church street.
Quin, — smith and farrier, Irish street.
Quin, Thomas, blacksmith, Market street.
Quin, John, blacksmith, Irish street.
Quin, Patrick, carrier, School-house lane.
Quin, P. huxter, Irish street.
Quin, Patrick, huxter, Scotch street.
Quin, Matthew, mason, Chapel yard.

R

Ramsey, Nathaniel, gent. Market street.
Rice, James, hatter, Ann street.
Richardson, Leander, printer and stationer, Market street.
Richardson, Lewis, printer, bookbinder and stationer,
    Church street.
Roberts, M. stay-maker, Perry street.
Robinson, Mrs. Market street.
Robinson, Joseph, carpenter.
Rogers, Miss, Scotch street.
Rogers, William, grocer, Perry street.
Rogers, Hugh, tailor and habit-maker, Market st.
Rogers, Michael, tailor, Irish street.

S

Shaw, Edward, Esq. bleacher, *Castlecaulfield.*
Shaw, John, merchant, *Dree.*

Sheals, Daniel, huxter, Irish street.
Shiel, James, barrister at law, *Lakefield.*
Shields, Robert, Esq. *Ivy Cottage.*
Shuter, John, Esq. Northland row.
Simmons, C. and R. grocers, Scotch street.
Simmons, Charles, grocer, Scotch street.
Simonton, Henry, publican, Church street.
Sinclair, John, surgeon, dispensary.
Sinclair, James, publican, Irish street.
Skeffington, B. shoemaker, Irish street.
Skeffington, John, shoemaker, Scotch street.
Small, William, baker, Market street.
Smith, Robert, grocer and ironmonger, Market st.
Smith, Eliza, grocer, Church street.
Smith, Thomas, cabinet-maker & upholsterer, Scotch street.
Smith, James, spindle-maker and whitesmith, Irish street.
Smith, Charles, slater, George's street.
Sproul, Mrs. School-house lane.
Staples, Rev. Alexander, *Mullaghmore.*
Steel, Samuel, shoemaker, Perry street.
Steenson, John, reedmaker, Scotch street.
Steenson, John, tailor, Irish street.
Stuart, Hon. A. G. *Lisdoae.*
Stuart, Alexander, Esq. *Drumreagh.*
Stuart. Miss, Scotch street.
Stuart, John, carpenter, Market street.

T

TALLON, James, dristributor of stamps, Perry st.
Tener, Robert, linendraper, Perry street.
Tennant, William, *Friendship Tavern,* Market st.
Thompson, John, attorney, Northland row.

Tipping, Henry, bookbinder, Church street.
Trotter, Wesley, grocer and spirit merchant, Market street.
Turkington, John, boot and shoemaker, Church st.
Turner, Jonathan, linendraper, School-house lane.

V

VANCE, Oliver, woollendraper and haberdasher, Market
  street.
Verner, William, Lieutenant-Colonel, *Churchhill.*

W

WALLACE, Hugh, innkeeper, *Northland Arms,* Market street.
Walsh, William, Captain, *Beech Valley.*
Walsh, David, music master, Scotch street.
Ward, John, huxter, Irish street.
White, John, boot and shoemaker, Market street.
White, Thomas, boot and shoemaker, Market st.
Whittle, William, surgeon, *Milltown.*
Willcocks, Joshua, Esq. *Beech Valley.*
Wilson, John, Esq. Perry street.
Wilson, Loftus, innkeeper, Irish street.

Y

YOUNG, James, Esq. *Annaghinny.*

The Bank of England

THIS National Establishment took place by Act of Parliament, in the 5th and 6th years of the reign of William and Mary. The charter of their incorporation was dated July 27th, 1694. Their principal business is dealing in bullion of gold and silver, discounting bills, advancing money to the public on the credit of Acts of Parliament, circulating their own notes, &c. and exchequer bills for Government, besides the management of the public funds, which are immediately under their care, and constitute the National Debt.

Persons having discounting accounts, may discount Inland Bills of Exchange above £20 value, accepted payable at banking houses, every day in the week. They are left at the Discount Office before twelve o'clock, and the answer is given at two.

Town notes or bills of above £100 each, accepted payable at banking houses are discounted only once a-week, and are left before twelve on Wednesdays, and the answer is given after one o'clock on Thursdays. No private account can be opened at the Drawing Office of the Bank of England, except on a first deposit of £500.

London Bankers.

BARCLAY, Tritton, Bevan, & Co. 54, *Lombard-street.*
Barnard, Dimsdale, & Dimsdale, 50, *Corn-hill.*
Biddulph, Cocks, Ridge, & Co. 43, *Charing Cross.*
Birch & Chambers, 160, *New Bond street.*
Bond, John, Sons & Patisal, 2, *Change Alley, Cornhill.*

Bosanquet, Pitt, Anderson & Franks, 73, *Lombard-street.*

Bouverie & Antrobus, 55, *Craven-street, Strand.*

Brooks, Son & Dixon, 25, *Chancery-lane.*

Browne, Langhorn & Bralsford, *Bucklersbury.*

Chatteris, Whitmore & Co. 24, *Lombard-street.*

Child & Co. 1, *Fleet-street, Temple-bar.*

Coutts, Thomas & Co, 59, *Strand.*

Curries Raikes & Co. 29, *Cornhill.*

Curtis, Roberts & Curtis, 15, *Lombard-street.*

Dorrien, Magens, Dorrien & Mello, 22, *Finch-lane, Cornhill.*

Drummond Andrew, B. John, and Charles & Co. 49, *Charing-cross.*

Esdaile, Sir James, Knt. Esdaile, Esdaile, Hammet & Hammet, 21, *Lombard-street.*

Everett, Walker, Maltby, Ellis & Co. 9, *Mansion-house-street.*

Frys and Chapman, *St. Meldred's court, Poultry.*

Fuller, Richard and George & Co. 84, *Cornhill.*

Gill, Thomas, & Co. 42, *Lombard-Street.*

Glyn, Sir Richard Carr, Bart. Mills, Halifax, Glyn & Co. 12, *Birchin-lane.*

Goslins& Sharpe, 19, *Fleet street.*

Grote & Prescott, 62, *Threadneedle-street.*

Hanbury, Taylor & Lloyds, 60, *Lombard-street.*

Hankey, Hankey & Co. 7, *Fenchurch-street.*

Hammersleys, Greenwood. Drew & Brooksbank, 76, *Pall-mall.*

Herries, Farqahar & Co 16, *St. James's-street.*

Hoare, Henry, Henry Hugh, Charles, William Henry, and Henry Meyrick Hoare, 37, *Fleet-street.*

Hoare, Barnets, Hoare & Co. 62, *Lombard-street.*

Hodsoll & Stirling, 345, *Strand.*

Holt, William, 60, *Old Broad-street.*

Hopkinson, G. C. C. & E. 5, *St. Alban's-street.*

Jones, Lloyd & Co. 43, *Lothbury.*

Jones, John, 18, *West Smithfield.*

Kinlock, J. F. & Sons, 1, *New Broad-street.*

Ladbrokes, Thornton & Gilman, *Bank buildings, Cornhill.*

Lees, Brassey & Farr, 71, *Lombard street.*

Lubbock, Sir John, Forster & Clarke, 11, *Mansion-house-street.*

Marsh, Sibbald, Stracey & Fauntleroy, 6, *Barner-street, Oxford-street.*

Marten, Call and Co. 25, *Old Bond-street.*

Martin, Stone & Martin, 68, *Lombard-street.*

Masterman, Peters Mildred, Masterman & Co. 2, *White Hall court, Lombard-street.*

Merle & Co. 2, *Cox's court, Little Britain.*

Morland, Ransom & Co. 56, *Pall-mall.*

Nicholson, T. and S. Janson & Co. *Abchurch-lane.*

Pares & Heygate, 63, *Aldermanbury.*

Paxtons, Cockerell, Trail & Co. 57, *Pall-mall.*

Perring, Sir John, Bart. Shaw, Barber & Co. 72, *Cornhill.*

Pocklington & Lacy, 60, *West Smithfield.*

Pole, Sir Peter, Thornton, Free, Down & Scott, 1, *Bartholomew-lane.*

Preads, Mackworth & Newcombe, 189, *Fleet-street.*

Price, Sir Charles, Bart. Kay, Price & Chapman, 1, *Mansion-house-street.*

Rogers, Towgood & Co. 29, *St. Clement's-lane, Lombard-st.*

Sharpe & Sons, 8, *West Smithfield.*

Sansom & Postlethwaite, 65, *Lombard-street.*

Sikes, Snaith & Co. 5, *Mansion-house-street.*

Smith, Payne & Smiths, *George-street, Mansion-house.*

Snow, Robert, William Sandby, John Dean Paul, & Snow, 217, *Strand.*

Spooner, Attwoods & Co. 27, *Gracechurch-street.*

Stehpensons, Remingtons, Smith & Co. 69, *Lombard-street.*
Stevenson & Salt, 80, *Lombard-street.*
Veres, Baron & Co. 77, *Lombard-street.*
Wentworth, Chaloner & Rishworth, 25, *Threadneedle-street.*
Weston, Pinhorn, Newsome & Weston, 37, *Borough.*
Willis, Percival & Co. 76, *Lombard-street.*
Williams, Son, Moffat & Burgess, 20, *Birchen-lane.*
Wright, Selby & Robinson, 5, *Henrietta-street, Covent-garden.*

Bank of Ireland.

(Established by Act of Parliament in 1783.)

Governor, Nathaniel Sneyd, Esq. 34, Sackville-street.
Deputy Governor, Arthur Guinness, Esq. 33, Granby-row.

DIRECTORS.

Robert Alexander, Esq.
Robert Ashworth, Esq.
James Chambers, Esq.
Leland Crothwait, Esq.
George Drevar, Esq.
Joseph Goff, Esq.
Arch. Hawksley, Esq.

Nathaniel Hone, Esq.
William P. Lunell, Esq.
William Snell Magee, Esq.
John Leland Maquay, Esq.
William Sparrow, Esq.
John Stewart, Esq.
Hugh Trevor, Esq.

Note.—The Directors are annually chosen the first week in April, under this restriction, that five new Directors be chosen every year.

OFFICERS.

Thomas William, *Secretary.*
William Dunlevy, *Acct. Gen.*
Nathaniel Low, *Cashier.*
E. Medlicot, *Chief Book-keeper.*
G. Draper, *chief Clk. of Discts.*

Brab Stafford, *Transfer officer.*
D. Houghton *chief clk of Deb.*
J.Gibons, R. Williams *Notaries.*
Fleetwood & Darley *Law Agts.*
James Draper, *Stationer.*

Close Holidays, Good-Friday, King's birth-day, and Christmas-day.

Days of Discount, every day except Saturday.—The Board meets every Tuesday.

BANKERS OF DUBLIN.

Alexander, Sir William, Bart. Robert Alexander, jun. William James Alexander, and William Johns Alexander, Esqrs. *Upper Sackville-street.*

Ball, Benjamin, Matthew James Plunkett, Philip Deyne, jun. and Henry Samuel Close, Esqrs. *Henry-street.*

Finlay, Thomas, John Geale, Robert Law, and Michael Law, Esqrs. *Jervis-street.*

La Touche, George, J. D. La Touche, J. La Touche, jun. P. La Touche, jun. P. D. La Touche, and James D. La Touche. Esqrs. *Castle-street.*

Newcomen, Right Hon. Viscount, and James Evory, Esq. *Castle-street.*

Shaw, Robert, T. Needham, and P. Shaw, Esqrs. *Foster-place.*

IRISH PROVINCIAL BANKERS.

Who Registered in 1818.

Belfast,	D. Gordon, N. Batt, J. H. Houston, and H.Crawford Esqrs.
Belfast,	William Tennent, Robert Calwell, Robert Bradshaw, John Cunningham, and John Thompson, Esqrs.
Belfast,	Hugh Montgomery, John Hamilton, James Orr, and John Sloan, Esqrs.
Carrick-on-Suir,	Richard Sauce, Esq.
Clonmel,	William Rial, Charles Rial, and. Arthur Rial, Esqrs.
Cork,	Joseph Pike, Esq.
Cork,	Sir Walter Roberts, Bart. Charles H. Leslie, and John Leslie, Esqrs.
Cork,	Stephen and James Roche, Esqrs.
Kilkenny,	James Laughnan, Esq.
Limerick,	Thomas and William, Roche, Esqrs.
Limerick,	George Evans, Esq. Jonath. & G. Bruce, Esqrs.
Lurgan,	Joseph Malcomson, Henry M'Veigh, & Alex. Cuppage, Esqrs.
Mallow,	Robert De La Cour, and R. T. Cuthbert, Esqrs.
Tipperary,	Dennis Scully, and James Scully, Esqrs.
Waterford,	William, Samuel, and John Newport, Esqrs.
Waterford,	T. Scott, G. Ivic, Robert, George, and Henry Scott, Esqrs.
Wexford,	John Redmond, Esq.
Wexford,	Nic. C. Hore, & Chas. Henry Hatchell. Esqrs.

THE END

OTHER TITLES FROM BOOKS ULSTER

Fighters of Derry: Their Deeds and Descendants, Being a Chronicle of Events in Ireland during the Revolutionary Period, 1688–91

William R. Young

ISBN 978-1910375082

Annals of the Famine in Ireland, in 1847, 1848, and 1849

Asenath Nicholson

ISBN 978-1910375631

Ireland's Welcome to the Stranger

Asenath Nicholson

ISBN 978-1910375624

My Lady of the Chimney Corner

Alexander Irvine

ISBN 978-1910375327

Betsy Gray or Hearts of Down: A Tale of Ninety-Eight

W. G. Lyttle

ISBN 978-1910375211

Daft Eddie or the Smugglers of Strangford Lough: A Tale of Killinchy

W. G. Lyttle

ISBN 978-1910375235

Made in the USA
Monee, IL
11 June 2020